D1002048

SCHOOL OF THEATRE

Garland English Texts

Stephen Orgel
Editor

Jerome McGann
Associate Editor

THE OLD LAW
by Thomas Middleton
and William Rowley

edited by
Catherine M. Shaw

Garland English Texts
Number 4

GARLAND PUBLISHING, INC.
NEW YORK & LONDON
1982

Library of Congress Cataloging in Publication Data

Middleton, Thomas, d. 1627.
  The old law.

  (Garland English texts ; no. 4)
  Bibliography: p.
  I. Rowley, William, 1585?–1642?   II. Shaw,
Catherine M.   III. Title.   IV. Series.
  PR2714.042   1982   822′.3   82-880
  ISBN 0-8240-9404-2   AACR2

Printed on acid-free, 250-year-life paper
Manufactured in the United States of America

Contents

Acknowledgments

I am grateful to the directors and staffs of the British Library, the Folger, Huntington, and Newberry Libraries for their unfailing help and cooperation and to Professor Virginia Carr for her assistance in reading proof and for making helpful textual comments. In particular, I would like to thank the British Library for permission to print the title page of the 1656 Quarto of *The Old Law* held in the Ashley Library.

Catherine M. Shaw
Concordia University
Montréal, Canada

Abbreviations

Bentley	G.E. Bentley, *The Jacobean and Caroline Stage*, 7 vols. (Oxford, 1941–68)
Chambers	E.K. Chambers, *The Elizabethan Stage*, 4 vols. (Oxford, 1923)
CHEL	*Cambridge History of English Literature*, 15 vols. (Cambridge, 1919–1930)
DNB	*Dictionary of National Biography*, (London, 1885–99)
Greg	W.W. Greg, *A Bibliography of the English Printed Drama to the Restoration* (Oxford, 1939–59)
HLQ	*Huntington Library Quarterly*
MLN	*Modern Language Notes*
MLR	*Modern Language Review*
MP	*Modern Philology*
OCD	*Oxford Classical Dictionary* (Oxford, 1970)
ODEP	*Oxford Dictionary of English Proverbs* (Oxford, 1970)
OED	*Oxford English Dictionary*, 13 vols. (Oxford, 1933)
Partridge	Eric Partridge, *A Dictionary of Slang and Unconventional English* (London, 1937)
PMLA	*Publications of the Modern Language Association*
RES	*Review of English Studies*
SP	*Studies in Philology*

SR	*A Transcript of the Registers of the Company of Stationers of London*, Edward Arber 1554–1640, 5 vols. (London, 1875–77; Birmingham, 1894); G.E.B. Eyre and C.R. Rivington, 1640–1708, 3 vols. (London, 1915)
STC	*A Short Title Catalogue of Books Printed in England, Scotland, & Ireland and of English Books Printed Abroad*, A.W. Pollard and G.R. Redgrave 1475–1640, 2 vols. (London, 1926); Donald Wing 1641–1700, 6 vols. (New York, 1945)
Tilley	M.P. Tilley, *A Dictionary of the Proverbs in England in the Sixteenth and Seventeenth Centuries* (Ann Arbor, 1950)

INTRODUCTION

The Authors

Thomas Middleton, the older of the two dramatists who collaborated in the writing of *The Old Law*, was born in London in 1580 to Anne and William Middleton, a bricklayer of no small affluence. Although his father's death in 1586 and the subsequent legal disputes between his mother and new step-father, Thomas Harvey, caused some diminishing of the family assets, Middleton did attend Queen's College, Oxford, from 1598 until 1600. There is, however, no evidence he was ever granted a degree. In fact, a legal deposition dated February 8, 1601, which P. G. Phialas cites, states that "Thomas Middleton was forced by reason of some controversies betweene his mother and Allen Waterer [Middleton's brother-in-law] to come from Oxenforde to helpe his mother Anne Harvie when her husbonde was at Sea whereby he thinkethe he loste his Fellowshipp at Oxenforde." Another deponent, though disclaiming any actual knowledge of the loss of the fellowship, adds that he thinks it to be true for "nowe he [Middleton] remaynethe heare in London daylie accompaninge the players."[1] Thus, although Middleton had published some non-dramatic pieces before this date, *The Wisdom of Solomon Paraphrased* (1597), *Micro-Cynicon, Six Snarling Satires* (1599), and *The Ghost of Lucrece* (1600), by early 1601 he had chosen association with the theatrical set and in 1602 his name starts to appear in Henslowe's *Diary* linked with those of Munday, Drayton, Webster, and Dekker, other dramatists producing plays for the Admiral's company at the new Fortune theatre. It was also during this early apprenticeship period that the playwright met and married Maria, the sister of Thomas Marbeck, an actor with the Fortune company. It was not, however, Middleton's association with the Admiral's or his early hack work for Henslowe that gained him his first reputation as a writer of comedy. Rather, it was a group of independent, somewhat satiric plays, a number of them London comedies, which he wrote for Paul's Boys. Of these, *The Phoenix* (1603-4), *A Trick to Catch the Old One* (1604-7), *A Mad World, My Masters* (1604-7), and *Michaelmas Term* (1604-6) are extant. A fifth, *Your Five Gallants* (1604-7), may also belong to this group.

---

[1] "Middleton's Early Contact with the Law," *SP*, LII (1955), 191-2.

The years between 1606-7 and 1611 appear to be strangely unproductive ones for Middleton as an independent dramatist. The collapse of Paul's Boys, who disappear from theatrical records after June, 1606, may have contributed to this. However, Harold N. Hildebrand's proof that Middleton wrote the non-extant *The Viper and Her Brood* in late 1605 and perhaps *Your Five Gallants* (1604-7)[2] for the Children of the Queen's Revels indicates that the playwright had already transferred his allegiance to the rival company at Blackfriars before this. Yet the move was not immediately fortunate for the years following thrust one disaster after another upon the Queen's Revels. The scandal aroused by the Chapman, Jonson, Marston *Eastward Ho!* (1605) which cost the company its royal patronage was followed, as a result of further offence given by Day's *Isle of Gulls* (1606), by their temporary excommunication from the Blackfriars theatre. In 1608, the company, now called the Children of the Chapel or of the Revels, was again in trouble. Chambers cites one of the parts of Chapman's *Conspiracy and Tragedy of Byron* and another unnamed play as being the offenders (II, 53-4). Although the company did manage to rally from these setbacks and find new quarters at Whitefriars when the King's Men moved into Blackfriars, the whole unsettled atmosphere was hardly conducive to creativity.

It might also be noted that changes were occurring in the Admiral's company as well. The adult company had been, after the death of Queen Elizabeth in 1603, taken into the service of Prince Henry and came to be known by his name. Shortly after this, certainly by 1606, the name of Edward Alleyn, son-in-law of Henslowe and a king-pin in the company, had disappeared from its rolls (Chambers, II, 186-8). Apparently, though maintaining certain financial interests, he became inactive and actually removed himself from London. It may well be that the "new blood" which Chambers records as being introduced into the company between 1606 and 1610 was antipathetic to a dramatist whose work for them had been little more than piecemeal.

One way or another, Middleton's next plays were written for the Lady Elizabeth's Men, a company which in March, 1613, amalgamated with the new Children of the Queen's Revels, by now restored to royal favour. These were *A*

[2] "Thomas Middleton's *The Viper's Brood*," *MLN*, XLII (1927), 25-8.

Chaste Maid in Cheapside (1611-13) and *No Wit, No Help Like a Woman* (1613?). It was probably during his association with Lady Elizabeth's that Middleton came into contact with William Rowley with whom he later collaborated so successfully. In fact, the latter of these two plays, according to C. W. Stork, show comic touches which he assigns to Rowley's hand.[3] Indeed, although after 1615 Middleton wrote his independent plays for the King's Men, all five of the known collaborations between Middleton and Rowley were produced by Lady Elizabeth's or by Prince Charles' (I) which had, in turn, absorbed the principal members of Lady Elizabeth's by March, 1616 (Bentley I, 198-9). Among these was William Rowley who had been a principal member of Prince Charles' (I) company at least from 1609 when it carried the name of the Duke of York's Men.

Information about the life of William Rowley must be gleaned from theatrical or legal records associated with his stage career. Anything else is conjectural. Even his birth year, which Stork guesses to be 1585, is arrived at by working backwards from the first time Rowley's name is found in print.[4] Together with those of John Day and George Wilkins, his name appears on a dedicatory leaf inserted after the title-page late in the print-off of *The Travels of Three Brothers* (1607). Considering that this play, his collaboration with Heywood, *Fortune by Land and Sea* (1607-9), and, apparently, Rowley's own *A Shoemaker, a Gentleman* (1608) were presented by Queen Anne's Men, the assumption may be made that he started his theatrical career with the Curtain-Red Bull company.

Most of Rowley's career, however, 1609-1623, both writing and acting, was with the Duke of York's Men which became Prince Charles' (I) after the death of Prince Henry in 1612 and ultimately part of the Lady Elizabeth's-Prince's-Queen's Revels complex referred to above. Yet, perhaps somewhat ironically after such long loyalty, for the last two years of his life Rowley was attached to the King's Men for whom, among other things, he acted the part of the fat bishop in Middleton's *A Game at Chess* (1624). Bentley gives a listing of all the documented information on Rowley's life with both Prince's (I) and King's (II, 555-558; V, 1014-1018). Of particular importance in terms of

<hr>

[3] *William Rowley: His "All's Lost by Lust" and "A Shoemaker, A Gentleman,"* (Philadelphia, 1910), pp. 47-8.
[4] *ibid.* pp. 7-8.

his collaborations is the number of times his name appears as actor. It would appear that his experience in this capacity, as a practical man of the theatre, was a most valued contribution to the Middleton-Rowley plays.

Comic characterization and incident were Rowley's dramatic forte and in this capacity critics have detected his hand in no less than fifty plays.[5] Although Rowley did write one independent tragedy, *All's Lost by Lust* (1619), and his best-known collaboration with Middleton, *The Changeling* (1622), was also a tragedy, nearly all other extant plays in which he had a hand are comedies and the distinctive quality of his comic style is farce; sometimes outrageously overdone but rarely other than genuinely funny and well integrated into the themes and morality of the central dramatic movement. The broadness of Rowley's humour, particularly when juxtaposed with Middleton's incisive and cultured wit suggests the lusty roughness of the London streets. Indeed, the comic style of which he was so obviously a master may be a clue indicating a birth and rearing in the city and an earlier and closer association with the work-a-day life of the London theatre than documentary evidence has been able to support.

The third name which appears on the title-page of the 1656 edition of *The Old Law* is that of Philip Massinger. Just how much Massinger had to do with the play when it was originally conceived or to what extent he may have revised certain passages will be discussed under Collaboration. Here, it is merely interesting to note that particularly close association between the three playwrights is unlikely to have been before 1621-1625, those years in which Massinger wrote *The Maid of Honour, A New Way to Pay Old Debts, The Bondman, The Renegado,* and *The Parliament of Love,* plays certainly written for Lady Elizabeth's and presented at the Phoenix. Apart from his beginnings with Henslowe (1613-15), Massinger's writing career was, like Middleton's, primarily associated with the King's Men. All three, however, were only together with this company between 1623 and 1625, five years after the date now accepted for *The Old Law.* It is true that Middleton and Massinger both wrote for King's from as early as 1615-16 but *The Old Law* was most likely produced by Prince's-Lady Elizabeth's as were the other collaborations.

[5] See D. M. Robb, "The Canon of William Rowley's Plays," *MLR,* XLV (1950), 129-41.

Unlike Middleton and perhaps even Rowley, Philip
Massinger was not a Londoner but was born in Salisbury. His
baptismal date is November 24, 1583. Like Middleton, however, he did attend Oxford although again there is no record
of a degree being granted. A distinction which sets
Massinger quite apart from either of the other two is his
association, through his father, with the politically and
socially prominent Herbert family. Arthur Massinger, the
father, served both the second and the third Earls of
Pembroke. He was also a fellow of Merton College and a
member of Parliament; distinctions which would appear to
indicate a more sophisticated upbringing for the son than
either of the other two dramatists with whom his name is
associated. Indeed, the closeness in age of Philip Massinger
and William, the third earl, may suggest that the dramatist
came under the influence of Samuel Daniel, tutor in the
Herbert household family, clearly acknowledged in the
dedication of *The Bondman* (1624), is the most likely link
between Massinger and the London theatrical world. The
third earl, after succeeding to the title in 1601, showed
himself kindly disposed toward a number of dramatists, not
the least of whom was William Shakespeare and, indeed, it
was William Herbert's appeal which stood the King's Men in
such good stead at the time of the *Game at Chess* scandal
(1624).

Massinger's name first appears in theatrical documents
around 1613 when, apparently for no more than two years, he
was a writer for Henslowe. After that, except for the few
plays mentioned above as being written for Lady Elizabeth's,
his playwriting was connected with the King's Men; first
primarily as a collaborator with John Fletcher and later,
after Fletcher's death in 1625, as the regular dramatist
with this company.

Of the three, Massinger lived the longest. Rowley and
Middleton died within a year of each other in 1626 and 1627;
Massinger in March, 1640. Although Rowley was active to the
end of his life as both dramatist and actor, Middleton's
contributions appear to have been abruptly curtailed after
the suppression of *A Game at Chess*. Apparently, once
Massinger took over Fletcher's place with the King's Men he
did no more collaborating. He did some revising of earlier
King's plays but mainly he produced an incredible number of
independent plays with such regularity that one might suspect him to be under some form of contract. His last play,
The Fair Anchoress of Pausilippo was licenced just a few

months before his death. Neither it nor *Alexius, or the Chaste Lover* which immediately preceded it are extant.

THE PLAY

The Date

In Act III of *The Old Law*, the parish clerk, in determining Agatha's age for her husband Gnotho, cites 1540 as the date of her birth and then continues, "and tis now '99" (III.i.29). Because of this comment, the play was long considering to have been first produced in 1599. Modern scholarship, however, on the basis of biographical, external, and internal evidence, has placed the play nearly twenty years later, in 1618.

In 1931, Professor Mark Eccles discovered a christening entry for April 18, 1580, in the Register of St. Lawrence Jewry, London, which reads, "Thomas sonn of will: Middleton." This, coupled with additional family information provided to the heralds by the playwright himself when they made their periodic visit to Surrey in 1623, led Professor Eccles to further evidence which proved conclusively that Thomas Middleton was born in 1580.[6] The playwright was thus unlikely to have collaborated in a play-making venture as early as 1599. In fact, he probably did not start writing plays until 1602 when he began producing pieces both for Paul's Boys and for the Admiral's. As far as William Rowley is concerned, nothing conclusive is known as to his birth date but again, considering that his name does not appear in any theatrical records until 1606-7, it is also highly unlikely that he took part in playwriting as early as 1599. The early dates referred to in the play are used, Professor Eccles contends, because of dramatic expediency rather than literal topicality. "Playwrights do not necessarily set their scenes in the current year of grace, and '99 is too obviously suitable a number for it to be taken literally as the date of composition." As for the year 1540, the clerk is persuaded by Gnotho to change the record so that Agatha's birth date will read 1539. "A writer for the study," Professor Eccles goes on, "would have chosen a birth-year easier for the clerk to alter, but the practical playwright preferred a round number to which his hearers could at once add sixty, the age of compulsory death."[7]

[6] "Middleton's Birth and Education," *RES*, VII(1931), 431.
[7] ibid. p. 433.

The title, "An ould Lawe . a . . . . ." appears in one of four play lists written on waste paper fragments which their transcriber, Frank Marcham, thinks were loosely inserted into a book probably made in 1619-20 by Sir George Buc, Master of the Revels 1610-22.[8] The fragments were subjected to fire and most titles are incomplete but it is possible that the missing part following "An ould Lawe" could have been "a new way to please you" the sub-title given in the 1656 quarto. E. K. Chambers, in his review of Marcham's publication, gave further support to this 1619-20 dating of Buc's book through a *Falstaff* entry on another fragment thus providing a fairly conclusive *terminus ad quem* for the writing of *The Old Law*. Chambers also adds, "It seems to me most likely that the lists represent plays which the Revels Office had at some time or another under consideration for performance at court." [9]

In terms of the *terminus a quo* the internal evidence for the 1618 dating is most conclusive. The specific evidence as well as other less impressive speculation is included by Professor Baldwin Maxwell in his *Studies in Beaumont, Fletcher, and Massinger*,[10] though he tends to discredit the inclusion of Massinger as co-writer of the play or even as a substantial reviser. There are two references within the play which place its writing almost certainly in 1618 and both of these occur in the one scene (ii, i) in which Simonides banters words with his father's serving men and finally discharges all of them as superfluous to his new life except the footman and the coachman. His reasons for keeping these two are explained in the dialogue:

> SIMONIDES   You have stood silent all this while,
> like men that know their strengths. In these
> days none of you can want employment [but] you
> can win me wagers, footman, in running races.
>
> FOOTMAN   I dare boast it, sir.
>
> SIMONIDES
> And when my bets are all come in and store,

---

8 *The King's Office of the Revels 1610-1622*, (London, 1925), pp. 3 and 15.
9 *RES*, I (1925), 484.
10 (Chapel Hill, 1939), pp. 138-46.

Then, coachman, you can hurry me to my whore.

(II.i.289-95)

In a letter to Sir Dudley Carleton, then ambassador to
Holland, dated April 10, 1618, John Chamberlain, that
Jacobean magpie who revealed so much about the reign of
James I, refers to a specific race between two footmen
which had London buzzing with excitement. The betting was
such that the Duke of Buckingham, Chamberlain tells his
friend, "went away with 3000li; and yt is saide for certain
there was more than twise as much won and lost that day."
"This story were not worth the telling," he goes on, "but
you may see we have litle to do when we are so far affected
with these trifles that all the court in a manner Lords and
Ladies (some further of, some neerer) went to see this race,
and the King himself as far as Barnet, and though the
weather were so sowre and fowle yet he was scant *fils de
bonne mere* that went not out to see, insomuch that yt is
verely thought there was as many people as at the Kings
first comming to London: and for the courtiers on horsebacke
they were so pittifully berayed and bedaubed all over that
they could scant be knowne one from another. Besides divers
of them came to have falles and other mishaps by reason of
the multitude of horses."[11] Such excitement and interest,
Chamberlain comments, will give Carleton some idea of the
"low ebbe" of London life when such "poor entertainments"
could cause such a stir. It was obviously such an event
that Simonides' reference to it would no doubt occasion
laughter.

After Simonides and the servants he intends to retain
leave the stage, the dialogue continues with a suggestion
from the butler of a way the others can mend their fortunes.
They can, he advises, seek out and marry widows of fifty-
nine. By then bearing with them until they turn sixty, the
servants will attain their wives' fortunes when the women
lose their lives under the provisions of Evander's new
edict. The cook greets this idea with great enthusiasm and
concludes the scene with, "Oracle butler! oracle butler! He
puts down all the doctors of the name!" (II.i.310-11).
William Gifford notes these lines to be an allusion to Dr.
William Butler (I, 38) an eccentric Cambridge physician who

11 *The Letters of John Chamberlain*, ed. N. E. McLure, vol.
2, *American Philosophical Society, Memoirs*, XII (1939), 155.

had, from about 1612, gained considerable London reputation for somewhat empirical diagnoses and cures. Fleay insists that the reference to the doctor in *The Old Law* indicates that the play must have been written before Butler's death January 29, 1618.[12] Gifford, on the other hand, points to evidence that the doctor's reputation continued for some years after his death. When, however, this allusion is coupled with the previous one, both coming within some twenty lines, a more likely conclusion is that *The Old Law* was written in late Spring or early Summer, 1618, when both incidents, the footmen's race and the death of Dr. Butler were fresh in the audience's mind. In that regard, of course, a further fillip to add to the foregoing evidence is that this dating places *The Old Law* squarely within the same period of time that other plays known to have resulted from the Middleton-Rowley collaboration were written.

The Collaboration

The partnership of Thomas Middleton and William Rowley in playwriting ventures was one of the most successful collaborations of the Jacobean era. Although each, at various times, had worked with other authors on joint theatrical productions, the combination of the efforts of the more scholarly and sophisticated poet, Middleton, with those of Rowley, dramatist, comic actor, and stock-holder in Prince Charles' (I) company, was a particularly happy one. The plays usually ascribed to this joint authorship are *A Fair Quarrel* (1617), *The Old Law* (1618), *The World Tossed at Tennis* (1619-20), *The Changeling* (1622), and *The Spanish Gypsy* (1623). (Concerning this last play, there is some controversy. Various critics have given it over either to John Ford or to Ford with a collaborator who may have been Middleton.)

There is no doubt that the uncertainty of how much, if at all, Massinger revised *The Old Law*, added to the corrupt state of the quarto text, has made it virtually impossible to assign with any surety each and every line of the play to its specific author. As R. H. Barker points out, "It is possible that what now looks like Rowley may sometimes be

---

[12] *A Biographical Chronicle of the English Drama: 1559-1642,* (London, 1891), II, 101.

corrupt Middleton or even corrupt Massinger."[13] George
Price sees strong evidence for Massinger's revising hand in
Act I, II.i, III,ii, IV.ii, and V,[14] whereas Barker is not
sure he was concerned in the play at all.[15]

Professor Barker is responsible for a fine summary of
all previous scholarship on the testy problem of authorship
and it is not necessary to repeat it in detail here.
Rather, the general statement can be made that in the
initial assemblage of ideas, Middleton appears to have been
responsible for the over-all structural and thematic unity
of the play and specifically for the court plots - the
serious involving Cleanthes-Hippolita-Leonides and the comic
of Simonides-Eugenia-Lisander. To Rowley, on the other hand,
belongs the farcical Gnotho plot and those sections which
integrate it into the main narrative such as the episode at
the end of II.i. in which Simonides' discharge of his
father's servants leads to actions which link their fate
with Gnotho's and his "venturing" schemes. Such a pun as
"Oracle butler! oracle butler!" could only belong to Rowley.
At the same time, however, it can be assumed that the more
fastidious Middleton would smooth over the rougher parts of
Rowley's work and Rowley lend his hand to increasing certain
comic elements. The parallel use of the double meaning
ascribed to "church book" on both the serious and the
farcical levels of the play would support this. The clever
double entendre is characteristic of Middleton's ironic
moralizing. The intellectualizing of a corruption which is
real and basic in the Gnotho plot, however, suggests that
the idea for the duality may have been Rowley's and that
Middleton elevated it from crassness to moral dignity.

Basing judgement in part upon what other scholars have
contributed in analyses of the stylistic idiosyncrasies of
each of the two playwrights, Act I clearly shows characteristics of both writers. Notwithstanding Barker's claim
based on rather slight evidence that the entire act is more
likely Rowley's, lines 1 - 128 appear to be more distinctively Middleton. The repeated legal references and the
biting riducule of legal sophistry is characteristic of the
older playwright as is the learning evident in the use of
allusions to Athenian law-makers and their judgements.

13 *Thomas Middleton,* (New York, 1958), p. 186.
14 "The Authorship and the Manuscript of *The Old Law,*" *HLQ,*
XVI (1953), 134.
15 *loc. cit.*

These lines also show a preponderance of pet phrases used by Middleton but rarely by Rowley: "pray you" and "prithee," "troth" and "by my troth," "faith" and "ifaith." Lines 220-542, on the other hand, include more linguistic devices characteristic of Rowley. His favourite expletive "tush" appears a number of times as do latinized words for which he showed proclivity: "vegetives," "reluctations," "ligaments of blood and propagation." Again there is a greater use of cliché in this part of the act. "Tyrant's sword," "sword of tyranny," "'tis tyranny that takes my life," as well as "unbosom my free conscience," appear within less than ten lines (11. 262-270). Pauline Wiggins in her fine early study, *An Inquiry into the Authorship of the Middleton-Rowley Plays*, points out that Rowley's serious characters are "worked out with entire absence of subtlety," that their motives "are much simpler than is natural." Although his women, she goes on, "show a nobility of character, an exalted virtue," they are romantic; "and indeed Rowley shows in all his serious work a tendency to romanticism which finds a parallel in the fantastic drollery of his comedies."[16] This is certainly true of both Hippolita and Cleanthes in this section of Act I. There is not a whit of humour in either of them nor does either show the slightest conflict of emotion or motive. As a result, although they are endowed with the highest of moral values, they lack humanity. In fact, Leonides' sense of the reality of his situation and his delight in the "sportive fine demur" made available by the plan to outwit the law, is of such a contrast to the other two that one might suspect some rewriting by Middleton's more subtle hand.

Act III scene i is perhaps the most difficult to assign in that characteristics of both authors appear much more narrowly interspersed. Lines 1 - 170 might be generally assigned to Middleton on the basis of the subtlety of wit and upon the intimate knowledge of courtly clothing styles and courtly affections. The construction of the verse, particularly in the longer speeches, has a smoothness not often achieved by Rowley. On the other hand, the ribaldry of Simonides' remarks to his mother (11. 121-125) and its continuance in the punning on "cast down" (11. 161-167) appear to be Rowley contributions. In four lines (146-149) there is an allusion to "cheese-trenchers" similar to one used by Middleton in *No Wit, No Help like a Woman's* (II.i. 60-69), followed by the kind of jest on flower names, in

[16] (Boston, 1897), pp. 15-17

this case on cheese rennet and Lady's Bedstraw, of which
Rowley was particularly fond. Barker assigns lines 192-194
to Rowley, pointing out their similarity to V.v.96-7 in his
All's Lost by Lust. Cleanthes' long speech (ll. 169-197),
he says, is probably Middleton's[17] although, judging from
the uneven quality of the verse, it could as well be Rowley's.
The pun "Oracle butler! oracle butler!" which ends the scene
has been mentioned above and those lines preceding the pun
(299-311) in which the butler divulges his plan to the
others are certainly Rowley's. The section in which
Simonides bandies words with his father's ex-servants might
have been written by either playwright.

The second scene of Act II is one of the three scenes
which most critics give principally to Middleton. There is
a sophistication of dialogue and a subtlety of characterization here which Rowley never achieved. The sexual punning
between Eugenia and her would-be wooers is based on a
glibness of tongue and whimsical exaggeration characteristic
of the more worldy Middleton. In fact, Eugenia is another
of Middleton's fine dissembling women such as are found in
Women Beware Women and in *More Dissemblers Besides Women*,
and the courtiers similar to those found in *Your Five
Gallants.* Perhaps, however, Rowley's hand can be seen in
the odd line. The parody from *Hamlet*, "Alas, poor ghost!"
(l. 82), is similar to the kind of thing he does with *2
Henry IV* and *Troilus and Cressida* in IV.i.

Only Acts III and IV can be divided between the two
collaborators with anything approaching certainty. The
first scenes of each of these two acts deal exclusively with
the Gnotho plot and abound with stylistic devices and language preferences distinctively Rowley's. In the opening
sequence of Act III, for example, the Pollux-Bollux obscenity and the assumed pedantry of the parish clerk are
typical Rowley audience pleasers. Indeed, although corrected
in this edition, the use of *Scirophon* for *Scirophorion* and
Hecatomcaon for *Hecatombaeon* (III.i.88) may have been in-
tentional, although it seems rather unlikely that the Jacobean
audience would have been familiar with Greek month-names.
Haberdepoise for *Avoirdupois* (IV.i.78), on the other hand,
would most certainly catch the audience's ear and be a
laugh line. Rowley's delight in grammatical jokes is seen
when he calls Ag "Thou preter-pluperfect tense of a woman"
(III.i.141). Again, the use of what D. M. Robb calls "cue-

17 *op. cit.* p. 187.

catching" lines,[18] such as appear in the repartee between
Gnotho and the serving men in both III.i. and IV.i. and
between Gnotho and the wine-drawer in IV.i., are clearly a
Rowley dialogue characteristic. In fact, when the two
scenes of each of these acts are compared, the main distinction between the comic styles of Middleton and Rowley
quickly becomes evident. As Pauline Wiggins pointed out,
where Rowley gives us "drollery and horse-play, Middleton
gives us wit and satire."[19]
        The humour of Middleton's scenes, the second in each of
Acts III and IV, depends primarily on verbal wit. Even
though Lisander goes through his "horse-trick[s]" in III.ii.
with attempted agility, the emphasis is on the ribaldry of
the dialogue; the punning on "whore's-trick" and the in-
terplay of human and animal sexuality. The challenges
which Lisander issues to the impertinent courtiers – dancing,
fencing, and drinking – are executed with stage action only
verging on farce when Simonides fails to show a strong
stomach, and even here decorum is maintained by the aris-
tocratic nature of the challenges themselves and by the
"court rules" which the courtiers, for all their audacity,
are willing to follow. There is again here the sophisticated finesse for which Middleton comedy is noted. In
fact, a comparison between these performances and those of
Gnotho or of Ag and the other old women attempting masque
dances in the scene immediately following (IV.i.) point up
clearly the differences in the comic styles of the two
authors. The difference is again shown in Cleanthes' dialogue with Eugenia at the close of the scene, in which he
shows flashes of temper at her jibes which somewhat enliven
his stodginess of manner under Rowley's hand. This distinction is again recognizable in his opening speech for
Act IV.ii. His fearfulness and his dialogue with himself on
cowardice allow for a character variability not previously
seen. The same might be noticed in the differences in
language and style in this scene. The speeches of Evander,
for example, show a similarity of metrical control com-
parable with his speeches assigned to Middleton in Act II.
In addition to these generalizations on the two Middleton
scenes discussed here, Barker provides a number of metaphoric parallels between specific lines in *The Old Law* and
passages from other Middleton plays.[20]

18 *op. cit.* p. 133.
19 *ibid.* p. 22.
20 *op. cit.* pp. 187-9.

Price and Barker assign the whole of Act V to Rowley and, certainly, the frequent use of rhymed couplets, the awkwardness of the blank verse, and the bluntness of the humour of the Gnotho sequence would indicate they are right in their general assessment. In addition, however, this act was probably the most botched in the copy text. There is barely a passage wherein some error in text is not flagrant - speeches misapplied, words obviously misreadings by the printer, and so on. It might also bear the strongest evidence for Massinger revisions, although in spite of the confidence with which Price[21] and Robb[22] assign lines to Massinger's revising hand, their differences with each other testify to the fallibility of attempting such specificity. Or, again, Hippolita's speeches (V.i.57-63, 66-77) are, according to Price, distinctive of Massinger's "sentiment and rhythm."[23] There is, however, a dignity in this passage and an evenness of style which might as easily indicate a Middleton revision of moral sentiments characteristic of Rowley. The Gnotho sequence, then, is certainly almost pure Rowley. The rest of Act V appears to have been originally by Rowley with considerable rewriting by Middleton. And Barker is probably right when he concludes that little evidence points to Massinger having any definite part in the play at all either in this act or in any other of the play. Emil Koeppel is adamant on this point. "No trace," he says, "of his [Massinger's] individual style is to be discovered in the existing text.[24]

Early Performances

Although there is no documentary evidence for any specific performance of *The Old Law*, there is no reason to doubt that when Middleton and Rowley set about their collaboration the play was intended for presentation immediately upon completion. We can assume, therefore, that it first appeared upon the boards in the late Spring or early Summer of 1618 (see above pp. xi-xiv). This date is too late for Prince's (I) to have been at the Hope theatre and

21 *op. cit.* pp. 132-3.
22 *op. cit.* p. 137.
23 *op. cit.* p. 133.
24 *op. cit.* CHEL VI, 145

too early for them to have moved, with Christopher Beeston, to the Phoenix (1619). Thus, if Bentley's conjectures are right (I, 201-3), the Prince's (I) occupied the Red Bull during this interim from 1617 until 1619 and presented *The Old Law* at that theatre.

The inclusion of *The Old Law* among others, including another Middleton-Rowley collaboration *A Fair Quarrel*, in a list which Chambers suggests may represent plays being considered for court presentation can perhaps be construed as slight evidence pin-pointing another possible performance in 1619-20 (see above p. xii). Even its consideration for such an honour, however, would seem to indicate its success in the public theatre. (If Philip Massinger was called upon to revise *The Old Law*, presumably after 1626-27, this may also be some evidence of the play's initial popularity. It is hardly likely that an unsuccessful play would have been considered for revival or that it would have been turned over to as respected a dramatist for this task if some guarantee based on past performances were not assumed.)

The title-page of the 1656 quarto presents another conundrum. It states that the play was "Acted before the King and Queene at *Salisbury House*, and at severall other places, with great Applause." The Salisbury Court Theatre, built in 1629, was still standing at the bottom of what is now Dorset Street at the time of the printing and would surely have been named correctly had this site been intended. *Salisbury House* more likely refers to the home of Edward Sackville, Earl of Dorset, who did, in fact, entertain Charles and Henrietta-Maria a number of times at his home in Salisbury Court. Although Bentley mentions some speculations on the specific occasion, there is again no real documentary evidence to support a particular instance (IV, 891). As for the "severall other places," this may indeed be the truth and indicate various performances but it may also be, as the placing of Massinger's name at the head of the authors, publisher's license to promote sales.

Finally, William Gifford makes a comment in his Introduction to Massinger's *Works* which is more frustrating than informative. In addition to *The Bondman* and *The Roman Actor*, he says he "can find but two more of Massinger's plays which were acted in the period following the Restoration, *The Virgin-Mary* and *The Renegado*; I have, indeed, some idea that *The Old Law* should be added to the scanty list; but having mislaid my memorandums, I cannot affirm it" (I.lvi-lvii).

The Sources

Further research into the sources of *The Old Law* has not revealed anything beyond what was originally discovered by Karl Christ in 1902,[25] by Thomas Cranfill in 1959,[26] and then added to by Professor David George in his doctoral dissertation "A Critical Study of Middleton's Borrowings and of his Imitations of other Authors in his Prose, Poetry and Dramatic Works."[27] To these men most of the following information is due. I am particularly grateful to Professor George for giving English paraphrases and elaborations on Christ's study and for information on specific plot detail from various possible source texts which are particularly rare.

The main plot involving Evander, his edict, and its effect on his court comes from a version of *The Seven Sages* or *The Seven Wise Masters of Rome* translated from the Greek by the mediaeval monk Jean de Hauteseille (*Historia septum sapientum*, ca. 1200). How Middleton came by the tales is uncertain but the coincidence of specific detail in *The Old Law* and the tale of the third master in de Hauteseille is such that it excludes other possible similar versions such as *Libro Di Novelle, Et Di Bel Parler Gentile,* a collection edited by Carlo Gualternuzzi in 1572. The English chapbooks of the cycle are generally based on the Latin original; perhaps Middleton picked up the tale from one of these. The name Evander is mentioned in the *Geography* of Strabo (45 B.C. - A.D. 25) as that of a Greek who brought a colony from Arcadia during the founding of Rome but, as Professor George points out, Middleton shows in *Micro-Cynicon* that he knew enough Greek to put names together in it and the name may be simply Eu-andros or "good man".[28] Other details may have an earlier source in *De Verborum Significatione* by Marcus Verrius Flaccus (extant only in an abridgement made by Sextus Pompeius Festus in the 2nd or 3rd century A.D.) which Middleton may have known from its edition by Joseph Scaliger in 1576. There is little doubt, however, that Middleton's immediate source was the tale as it had come down from Jean de Hauteseille.

[25] *Quellenstudien zu den Dramen Thomas Middletons*, (Borne-Leipzig), pp. 100-104.

[26] *Rich's Farewell to Military Profession: 1581*, (Texas, 1959), p. xi.

[27] (University of London, 1966), pp. 193-206, [28] *ibid.* p. 197

Briefly, de Hauteseille's story deals with a youthful
monarch who, concerned for the economic strife brought upon
his realm by a long siege, takes the advice of his young
and selfish courtiers and passes a law ordering the deaths
of all men and women of sixty years because they are no
longer able to serve the realm and are also shortening the
supply of food for those who are. In this tale, it will be
noted, a specific reason is given for the edict whereas in
The Old Law the measure is passed, to all intents and purposes, on mere whim. It is also interesting to note that
all earlier sources set the execution age at sixty; only
Middleton changes the age for men to eighty. As de Hauteseille's story continues, only one old man is saved from
execution. Unlike others of the youthful counsellors, one
son defies the law and hides his father in a cave. The
son's wife, under oath, swears to keep the secret.

After the siege has been relieved, the injustice of the
initial edict spreads throughout the land and moral chaos
threatens. Again the young courtier who had hidden his
father emerges to defend the right. Gaining words of wise
counsel from his father, he passes on to the young King advice on rule by justice. Gradually his wisdom impresses his
monarch to the extent that he is elevated to the position of
a judge. At the same time, however, the unregenerate
counsellors have become resentful and plot against him.
Their suspicions lead to a plan whereby, on a public occasion, each subject will bring forth his best friend, his
worst enemy, his best jester, and his most faithful servant.
For the first of these, the scheming courtiers suspect the
faithful son will have to reveal his father. On the advice
of his father, the son first presents to the court his dog
as best friend, his ass as most faithful servant, and his
infant son as best jester. Then, no sooner has he named his
wife as his worst enemy than she proves to be just that.
Angrily she interrupts, calling upon evidence of all she has
done for him including the great care with which she has
served her father-in-law in hiding. Her husband immediately
points out that by her divulgence she has, indeed, proved to
be his worst enemy.

The young King, however, has gained wisdom under the
tutelage of the aged couseller and recognizes the planning
that has gone on. Rather than fulfilling the self-seeking
plans of the wicked counsellors, he pardons the young judge
for defying the unjust law and receives the father back into
the court with all honours. With this restoration, the

nation's reform is complete and wisdom and justice reign.
The plot cuts and thematic shifts which Middleton made
from his source reflect both the tastes of his age, and more
importantly, dramatic expediency. It is true that the idea
of a wise ruler wishing to test the moral fibre of his
nation, such as Duke Vincentio does in *Measure for Measure*,
was a popular one on the Jacobean stage, but dramatically speaking the removal of Evander from central partici-
pation in the action allows for the establishment of
greater shading in the reaction of character to situation.
Establishing Evander as overseer (and including the third
plot level - the farcical Gnotho plot), the play takes on
these character gradations:

                        EVANDER

CLEANTHES   HIPPOLITA   LEONIDES
    | | |
SIMONIDES   EUGENIA   LISANDER
    | | |
 GNOTHO   SIREN   OLD AG

Other changes from the original tale also remove the
emphasis from mere story to character diversity and moral
conflict. Hippolita, for example, has sworn no oath in *The
Old Law* and tells the family secret not in fit of pique but
as a result of genuine compassion, albeit misplaced. Or
again conundrums such as the challenge to produce best
friend, servant, jester, and worst enemy are plot gimmicks
common to the tradition of folk narrative but unnecessary
and, in fact, distracting once the dramatic interest has
been shifted to character and moral conflicts. Of course if
Evander is cast as the benevolent overseer he cannot be
responsible for actual death. Therefore, the old people
must merely be secreted away until their reappearance can
become part of the grand exposure and reformation at the
end of the play.
Apart from these and other cuts and changes, there are
also some additions to the narrative. In *The Old Law* there
are not only self-seeking sons anxious to be rid of aged
parents but also a young wife fretting to cast off an old
husband. In addition to the comic level which Eugenia and
Lisander bring to the play, their inclusion expands the
moral dimensions of the play beyond "Thou shalt not kill"
and "Honour thy mother and thy father" to include "Thou

shalt not commit adultery" and "Thou shalt not covet thy
neighbour's wife."

Middleton and Rowley called upon other incidental
sources in fleshing out the main narrative framework for
The Old Law. For the lawyers' citing of the judgements of
ancient law-makers in the opening sequence of the play,
Middleton drew upon Sir Thomas North's translation of
Plutarch's *Lives* of Lycurgus and Solon.[29] It is clear from
the text that for Cleanthes' use of the loyalty of Aeneas
to his father Anchises as an analogy with which to castigate
the false courtiers (V.i.219-231), Rowley has gone straight
to Virgil. Indeed, it may well be that Virgil's designation
of the "temple of Ceres" beside the ancient cypress as the
family meeting place in the *Aeneid*[30] led the lesser playwright to use a lodge within "thickets" in which Cleanthes
could hide his father (I.i.480-1) rather than the cave
designated in the de Hauteseille tale.

A parallel for the comic sub-plot of Gnotho and Agatha
was discovered by T. M. Cranfill to be the sixth tale of
[Barnaby] *Rich's Farewell to Military Profession* (1581)
which, in turn, came from Cinthio's *Hecatommithi* III.5.
Although in the Preface to his edition of Rich's work (1959),
Cranfill points out differences between the two tales, he
disclaims being able to tell whether Rowley's immediate
source was the English or the Italian version.[31] Professor
George, however, notes the greater similarity between the
name of Rowley's Gnotho and Rich's Gonsales than Cinthio's
Consalvo and adds that there is no evidence that Rowley
could read Italian. On the basis of this he opts for the
English source.[32]

The argument of Rich's tale "Of Gonsales and his ver-
tuous wife Agatha" is as follows:

> Gonsales, pretendying to poison his verteous wife
> for the loue of a Courtisane, craued the helpe
> of *Alonso* a Scholer somethyng practised in Phisicke,
> who in the steade of poyson gaue hym a pouder,
> whiche did but bryng her in a sounde sleepe
> duryng certaine howers, but *Gonsales*, iudgyng (in
> deede) that his wife had been dedde: caused her

---

29 For the specific legal terms used, see 1579 ed., p. 95
30 ed. Thomas Phaer (1573), F 1 .
31 *op. cit.* p. xl.
32 *op. cit.* pp. 203-4.

immediatly to be buried, The Scholer againe
knowyng the operation of the pouder for the
greate loue he bare to *Agatha*, went to the
vault where she was entombed, about the hower
that he knewe she would awake. When after some
speeches vsed betweene theim, he carried her home
to his owne house, where she remained for a space,
in the meane tyme *Gonsales* beeyng married to his
Courtisane, was by her accused to the Gouernour
for the poisoning of his first wife, whereof being
apprehend he confessed the facte, and was therefore iudged to dye, whiche beyng knowne to *Agatha*,
she came to the Iudge, & clearyng her housbande of
the crime, thei liued together in perfect peace &
amitie.

(p. 148)

In *The Old Law* each of the three main characters from
Rich's tale: Gonsales, Agatha, and the courtesan Aselgia,
have been, under Rowley's comic hand, transformed from
serious stature to objects of farcical humour and the entire
tone shifted from ethical instruction to bawdy mimicry. Of
course changes in plot detail were necessary, particularly
the adjustment of old Ag's age, the addition of Gnotho's
pseudo-legal scheme for her riddance, and the inclusion of
Simonides' ex-servants to provide further grist for Gnotho's
venture mill; but the centre of the hilarity of the farcical sub-plot is Gnotho himself, such a fine comic figure
that it might be suspected that Rowley wrote the part for
himself. The audacious confidence in his own unscrupulous
machinations is only matched by the clown's insistence at
the end that the failure of his whole venture is Evander's
fault for indiscriminately changing laws and thus gulling
his poor subjects. The sorrowful lament with which he
leads his frustrated procession off stage hardly suggests
the happy marital prognosis anticipated by Rich.

The Staging of the Play

There are really only three problems of staging in *The
Old Law*. Of these, two are minor. One is the positioning
of Eugenia, Simonides, and the other Courtiers when they

view the antics of Lisander with his Dancing Master (III.ii.
1-126) and the other the scene of Leonides' discovery in the
woods by Evander and his company (IV.ii.56-186). In the
first the young mockers either hide behind some stage prop
or are positioned in an upper stage and look down upon
Lisander. The former seems more likely the case as there is
a maximum of five lines between Simonides' burst of laughter
and Lisander seeing them and challenging them to weapons;
hardly enough time to move from an upper stage to the main
acting area. Or, perhaps, an inner stage was used, in which
case the upper stage would be free for the musicians who
provide the accompaniment for the first challenge - the
galliard - and the main area clear for the dances and for
the "horse trick[s]."

In the second instance, there is no reason for stage
props nor, for that matter, the use of an inner stage.
Cleanthes' lines at the opening of the scene establish that
the action is taking place in the woods in which he has
secreted his father (IV.ii.1-7) and there are fifteen lines
of dialogue (11. 170-85) to allow for a verisimilitude of
time in which Simonides and the Courtiers can exit, supposedly search out Lisander, and return to the stage with
him captive.

The third staging problem is indicated by Halliwell-
Phillips in the volume on Actresses among his *Literary
Scraps*33 in which he lists *The Old Law* as being an example
wherein the musicians performed out of their usual room or
place. During the mock-funeral for Leonides (II.i.170-243),
it is unlikely the musicians would be out of their usual
position. From the musicians' gallery they could provide
the recorder accompaniment for the procession indicated by
the stage directions and then later, with horns, sound the
flourish when Evander leaves the stage. Again in IV.i., the
musicians would be positioned above the main acting area
since room must be left on stage for the dances of the old
women as well as their on-stage audience. As indicated by
the Drawer, "Here are sweet wire-drawers" (IV.i.44), the
musicians are in full view providing a visual parallel to
the verbal punning which follows, and they are thus in the
musicians' gallery. Halliwell-Phillips is obviously referring to Gnotho's wedding-funeral procession in the last
act (V.i.406-602) in which the musicians are among the
celebrants. Not only are they part of the initial stage

33 Folger, M.S. W.b. 137-200.

directions but twice Gnotho refers to them specifically with
"Fiddlers crowd on, crowd on," and warns that no man should
stand in their way (11.406-7, 415-16). Cleanthes also comments that Gnotho and his troop "do march with music" (1.
437). Finally when all of Gnotho's hopes are dashed he
bids, "Fiddlers farewell" (1. 578). Since the musicians
were required earlier in the scene (1. 298) to provide the
symbolic music for the entrance of the old men who were
previously thought dead, they must indeed have descended
from the upper musicians' room to the main level to be
ready for their on-stage appearance during which Gnotho
receives his come-uppance. Ample time, ninety-four lines,
is provided for this move.

Critical Judgement

Although *The Old Law* appears to have been popular in
its time, only Charles Lamb, with rather sentimental enthusiasm, has since expressed liking for the serious plot.[34]
Professor Barker finds the central situation "wildly fantastic"[35] and Professor Schoenbaum sees it as one in which
any potential for expressing "Middleton's conception of a
mercilessly just universe" is abandoned in a superfluous
fifth act.[36] As for the Gnotho scenes, it is to A. H.
Bullen that the critic must turn for the only real ap-
preciation of Rowley's "genuine gift of humour." However,
he concentrates his attention only on the Gnotho episode in
the fifth act which is, in fact, just one of three very
important farcical scenes. After describing the last of
these fully, Bullen concludes, "There is nothing in
Massinger's or Middleton's plays to match the drollery of
this scene; but whoever has read Rowley knows what a rich
vein of whimsical humour he could sometimes discover" (I.xv-
xvii). Other scholarly approaches to *The Old Law* in terms
of qualitative judgement have been few and rarely compli-
mentary. W. Gifford, though disclaiming the farcical
sequences, included the play in his edition *The Plays of
Philip Massinger*. He calls it an "unfortunate comedy" and

34 *Specimens of English Dramatic Poets*, (London, 1808),
p. 453n.
35 *Thomas Middleton*, p. 101.
36 "Middleton's Tragicomedies," *MP*, LIV (1956-7), p. 13.

condemns the lighter scenes as "awkward movements of filth and dullness" (IV, 578). The last of the Gnotho scenes he sees as a crowd-pleaser. "The groundlings of those days," he says, "like the godlings of the present . . . have had but too much influence, at all times, over the managers" (IV, 568). A. C. Swinburne found a "sense of discord and inequality" in the play and referred to the "clumsiness and dullness of the farcical interludes."[37] Although Helene Bullock, in her article devoted to a reassessment of Middleton as a playmaker, is willing in some ways to praise Rowley, she still refers to his "addiction to supplying low-life scenes" and to his "roughness."[38] As for the modern critics, Schoenbaum lumps together the farcical and comic levels and calls them "preposterous,"[39] and Barker says the Gnotho scenes have "all the faults and a few of the merits of the Launce scenes in Shakespeare."[40]

Unfortunately both of these critics assume that *The Old Law* is a tragicomedy[41] and both place the thematic emphasis upon Hippolita. The Middleton scenes, which Barker sees as the core of the play, are, he says, "essentially concerned with tragic weakness. They tell the ironic story of the unfortunate Hippolita, who betrays herself and her family, but who is nevertheless always moved by the very highest motives."[42] Schoenbaum agrees and adds, "The disturbing discovery to which *The Old Law* leads is that feminine virtue, in spite of all its attractiveness, is really not virtue at all but weakness, and its consequences are no less deadly than those of evil."[43] Although these critics accept the basic premise that the dramatic representation of *The Old Law* is carried on three levels: serious, comic, and farcical, they isolate one incident - the unconscious betrayal of her father-in-law by the otherwise ideal Hippolita which serves primarily in terms of narrative pro-

37 *The Age of Shakespeare*, (London, 1908), p. 164.
38 "Thomas Middleton and the Fashion in Playmaking," *PMLA*, XLII (1927), 775.
39 *op. cit.* p. 11.
40 *op. cit.* p. 100.
41 Professor Schoenbaum seems to have changed his mind later for in his 1964 revision of *Annals of English Drama 975 - 1700* (Pennsylvania) he concurs with Harbage's original classification of *The Old Law* as comedy.
42 *op. cit.* p. 101.
43 *loc. cit.*

gression rather than total thematic impression - and concoct a central and controlling thesis from it. Such a view seems to conflict with the obvious tri-level structure of the play and ignores the basic conflicts upon which the moral theme and stratification are based. These critics can only dismiss the Gnotho scene from the fifth act as superfluous. They cannot reconcile this or any other of the farcical scenes to such a thematic interpretation. Nor, for that matter, can the serious Cleanthes-Leonides-Hippolita relationship be seen as anything but incidental to Hippolita's scene with Eugenia in which, out of compassion and only after finding justification, she reveals the plan for protecting Leonides from the injustice to which he is liable under Evander's iniquitous edict. Only a broader perspective of *The Old Law* can reconcile all three levels - all three situations in which a man-made law leads to a violation of those moral laws set down in Holy Writ or, alternatively, the insistence upon morality leads to illegality. The play, when seen from this point of view, becomes intelligible on all three levels, and the Gnotho scenes take their place as integral to the thematic development of the moral issues involved. Structurally, the play is a mixture of dramatic sub-genres, controlled by a straight serious action but enhanced by comedy and farce and, it will be seen, skilfully integrated masque and anti-masque. Although artistically it may fall somewhat short of the greatest comedies of the Jacobean period, thematically it deserves its place among dramas projecting high morality with less self-consciousness than most of its contemporaries.

Primarily, the thematic representation of *The Old Law* is based upon a conflict inherent within the deliberate ambiguity of the title - a conflict between the Old Law, a law concerning old people, as we might use the term Corn Laws or Poor Laws, which has been newly enacted by Evander, Duke of Epire, and the old law of Moses, "honour thy father and thy mother." Evander's edict would put to death those of the realm beyond the age of bearing arms or children - men at eighty and women at sixty. Simonides, one young courtier, supports the advantages of the secular law; Cleanthes upholds the principles of the old moral law. To increase his fortune, Simonides contrives to hasten his parents to their graves; Cleanthes uses his "filial faculties" to outwit the Duke's law and save Leonides by staging his mock funeral and secreting his father in a forest lodge.

The establishment of this conflict and the preparation for future intrigue takes all of Act I and the first scene of Act II. Once the dramatic dichotomy between secular law and Holy Writ is firmly fixed and the initial character contrasts delineated in terms of filial obligation, the comic level of the play takes over. Simonides, heady with the promise of luxury gained from the death of his father under the Old Law of Epire, advances to covet Eugenia, wife to Lisander whose life is also threatened by the new edict. Still another moral law is violated, "thou shalt not covet thy neighbour's wife," and the matter of marital obligation comes under scrutiny. The unity between the serious and comic levels is provided by Simonides who is at once disloyal son and willing cuckolder and by Hippolita and Eugenia as they represent loyalty and disloyalty in family and marriage. Ironically, the breaking of the law of the land becomes equated with love and compassion and the maintaining of the law with lust and self-interest.

Act III scene i is the first of three cleverly integrated scenes in which the clown Gnotho and his associates appear on stage. The play without its farcical level would, though less effective dramatically, still stand complete. There is no reason, for example, why Act III scene ii could not have followed directly after the close of Act II. In fact, the low comedy figures have little direct communion with the main plots. Gnotho, though designated as clown, is obviously not attached to the court as Evander knows nothing about him and Gnotho does not recognize the Duke. It is also obvious, however, that great care has been taken to provide structural and thematic integration for the low comedy with the other levels of representation. One of the authors, and I assume it to be Rowley as he would be most directly concerned with the integration of his farcical scenes, provided that the servants of Creon, Simonides' father, become the associates of Gnotho after they have been rudely fired by the self-centred young courtier (II.i.251-311). The co-authors also achieved remarkable parallels between Act I scene i in which Simonides and Cleanthes converse with the lawyers and Act III scene i in which Gnotho gulls the parish clerk. Simonides' quizzing of the lawyers parallels Gnotho's of the parish clerk just as the lawyers' ostentatious Latin does that of the Clerk's garbled Greek. In both scenes deliberate and skilful dualities of meaning are centred upon the "church-book" or parish chronicle and upon "overthrow" and "cast [off]". Between Cleanthes and the lawyers the following conversation ensues:

> CLEANTHES   And this suit shall soon be dispatched
> in law?
>
> 1 LAWYER   It is so plain it can have no demur,
> The church-book [parish chronicle] overthrows
> [is the guide for] it.
>
> CLEANTHES   And so it does,
> The church-book [Bible] overthrows [defeats or
> subverts] it if you read it well.
>
> (I.i.124-28)

Between Gnotho and the parish clerk the dualities centre
upon whether the clerk can "cast a figure." For Gnotho's
immediate purposes this means can the clerk design or change
a numerical symbol in the parish chronicle, the secular
life records; for Gnotho's long-term plan, however, it also
means can he provide the means whereby a human figure, old
Ag, can be cast off, an action which would violate the
records of moral law as found in the Bible (III.i.61-66,
101-103). Both lawyers and Clerk, it will be noted, receive payment for their services and, before their scenes
are over, Gnotho has Cook, Tailor, Bailiff, and Butler following his example just as Simonides has his fawning courtiers. Finally, and most obviously alike, are Simonides'
desire to get rid of his parents and Gnotho's desire to get
rid of his wife, Agatha.

In answer, then, to the suggestion that the farcical
scenes were interpolated without care for their connection
with the play proper, in which case they could have been
inserted anywhere between the scenes of the other two plots,
their actual placement shows more than casual concern for
their dramatic effectiveness. The first low comedy scene
occurs after two complete acts have been devoted to establishing and developing the basic and interconnected moral
conflicts of the drama. On the courtly level, Simonides
complies with the law by doing nothing; Cleanthes breaks
the law by acting to thwart it. Then, in Act III scene i,
contrapuntal to this main dramatic movement, Gnotho, on his
vulgar level, does both. He only too delightedly complies
with the law that will rid him of Agatha but he also acts,
unlawfully, to hasten his freedom by gulling the parish

clerk into altering Ag's birth date in the parish chronicle.
Cleanthes violates the letter of the Duke's edict and ad-
heres to the spirit of moral law as found in the church book
[Bible]; Simonides adhered to the letter of the Duke's law
as it was supported by evidence in the church book [parish
chronicle] and violated the spirit of moral law. Gnotho,
again, assimilates both actions. By violating or changing
the letter of the church book [parish chronicle], he violates the spirit of the church book [Bible]. Gnotho's
further actions also parallel, ironically, those of
Simonides, the courtier whom Gnotho, on his much lower level,
most closely resembles. Simonides, thinking himself well on
the way to fortune, turns to lusting after Eugenia; Gnotho,
thinking himself on the way to a young wench, turns to
betting to increase his fortune. Thus the scene also acts
as a subtle leveller of the actions of the two scoundrels.

The second low comedy scene (IV.i.), a nonsense masque,
is also strategically placed. First, it follows a mock
tourney in which Simonides and the other courtiers are
overcome by old Lisander, Eugenia's husband. In a comic
though desperate attempt to "overthrow" the laws of nature,
Lisander tries to "cast off" the infirmities of age and
prove himself potent against Eugenia's would-be wooers and,
indeed, though his victory is short-lived, he does tem-
porarily put them to flight. After the competition,
Cleanthes, distressed at his uncle's foolish attempts to
appear young, turns on Eugenia with the name of "whore" (III.
ii.298). The farce of the nonsense masque which follows
plays the changes on just this word and by doing so makes
visually more intense the licentiousness of the comic level
of the play, for here is Gnotho with *his* whore, engaged in
bawdy tavern revelry with his friends. Their gaiety is
Gnotho's premature celebration of the funeral of his first
wife and his marriage to the second. The clown, his low-
level courtesan, and his friends, are roaring out bawdy puns
when the drawer of the tavern presents "a consort of mad
Greeks." They desire, he says, "to enter amongst any merry
company of gentlemen goodfellows, for a strain or two." The
masquers are, of course, Agatha and the old wives which
Butler, Cook, Tailor, and Bailiff have procured in order to
gain their property after the edict has claimed their lives
and to enter them in what is, quite literally, a death-race
at which Gnotho is the track tout. After the masque dances,
each of the masked women takes out her own husband. With
the Cook's words, "Ay, so kind! Then every one his wench to

his several room. Gnotho, we are all provided now, as you are," the gulled men depart the stage leaving Gnotho with two women on his hands (IV.i.85-104). A further mocking extension of the masque pattern is completely integrated into the dialogue. The unmasking takes place when Gnotho chooses Siren, the courtesan, for his company and Agatha reveals her identity. The gift-giving is Gnotho's promise to Siren that she shall have two new gowns and the best of Agatha's to make "raiments for the working days" (IV.i.129). The promise of joy and good fortune common to the celebratory masque are parodied by Agatha's curses and Gnotho's forecast of her early death.

Purely as low comedy, the scene is remarkably successful and shows fine skill in the adaptation of the masque device. Gnotho's outrageous effrontery is matched by that of the women who attempt the stately movements of an entertainment form distinctively belonging to the court. Of greater importance, however, is the dramatic representation of the violation of still another moral law. The rogues who are Gnotho's cohorts, albeit they are to be thwarted, show a willingness to commit adultery and, as for the clown himself, he is not only willing but, considering that he exits from the stage with his bawd, might be assumed to be successful in his desire.

The mock masque is immediately followed by a delightful woodland interlude of family love and fidelity. Its religious imagery heightens the obvious contrast between this scene and the two previous and elevates even more the one family which follows the old laws of morality. Not only are Cleanthes-Leonides-Hippolita the visual representation of "honour thy father and thy mother that their days may be long upon the earth," but such references as "heavenly marriage" (IV.ii.50) also call to mind "what God hath joined together let no man put asunder." Act IV ends in apparent disaster for the group, however, for Eugenia, acting to avenge Cleanthes for calling her "whore," has betrayed their secret and Leonides is discovered. The old man is led away to be dispatched according to the edict and Cleanthes is taken prisoner to answer for his "contempt against the law" (IV.ii.299).

In the courtroom scene at the end of the play, the three levels of the drama are brought together in a finale which shows not only effective structure within itself but also successfully interlocks the serious, comic, and farcical representations into a common and traditional resolu-

tion for thematic comedy. The opening dialogue recalls the
first and main conflict of values. The prisoner, Cleanthes,
is, according to the courtiers, the enemy - he who would
conceal his father and protect him from the law. The judge,
Simonides, on the other hand, humbly thanks the Duke for
sending his parents "a-fishing" (V.i.23). Quickly following,
Eugenia enters and is promised a "lusty April" by Simonides
when she "shall no longer bosom January" (V.i.40-2). The
two central issues, family and marital loyalty and obligation, are set side by side as Hippolita warns the young
courtiers:

>   . . . if [you] crimson
> Your name and power with blood and cruelty,
> Suppress fair virtue and enlarge of old vice,
> Both against heaven and nature draw your sword,
> Make either will or humour turn the soul
> Of your created greatness, and in that
> Oppose all goodness, I must tell you there
> You're more than monstrous. In the very act,
> You change yourself to devils.

>   (V.i.69-77)

With the entrance of Evander, the rest of the act decidedly
takes on masque overtones. In fact, the action follows the
formal, elevated masque so closely as to make us suspect the
authors of deliberately relying upon contrast with the
earlier nonsense masque. The Duke takes his seat of state
to observe the proceedings. He hears what amounts to a debate between Cleanthes and Simonides as they represent "love
and duty" versus "unnaturalness in humanity" (V.i.263, 272).
Just as it appears Simonides holds the upper hand, Evander,
the superior authority steps in. The Duke is, at this
point, acting as Presenter to the masque:

> 'Tis time I now begin,
> [And] where your commission ends.
> Cleanthes, you come from the bar.
> Because I know you're severally disposed,
> I here invite you to an object will, no doubt,
> Work in you contrary effects.
> Music!

>   (V.i.292-8)

Leonides, Creon, Lisander, and the other old men who were
thought to have perished under the law, enter to loud
strains. Although there are no real measures, one of the
courtiers, in amazement, refers to the sudden reversal as
"fine dancing" (V.i.314). The Old Law is replaced by
humane and just statutes by which power and wealth will
depend upon maturity in "obedience, manners, and goodness;"
sons thinking themselves ready for inheritance will be
judged on fitness by Cleanthes according to their "duty,
virtue, and affection;" wives who "design the[ir] husbands'
death" shall not marry for ten years after; and those who
would "entertain suitors in their husbands' lifetime" shall
be "judge[d] and censured by Hippolita, wife to Cleanthes"
(V.i.345ff).

The scene is just drawing to a fine and traditional
close with Evander's blessing of Cleanthes and Hippolita
with fortune and increase when, suddenly, to harsh music,
the low comedy figures enter replete with fiddlers and
bride's cake. Critics who have viewed the farce of *The Old
Law* as extra-dramatic would have the play end at the close
of the court scene, yet, in fact, if the masque parallel is
extended, this comic intrusion is in the correct position
for a second antimasque -- after the resolution of the plot
conflict and before the final dances.[44] And, as the farce
again provides counterpoint for the main plot, it fulfills
the essential purpose of antimasque by pointing up by contrast the beauties of harmony and reconciliation seen in
the conclusion of the main action which follows.

Gnotho and his friends have arrived for what they
think will be wedding celebrations -- his to Courtesan and
Agatha's to the hangman. Gnotho's farcical audaciousness
provides fine comic juxtaposition to the previous court
proceedings while, at the same time, focusing audience
attention on the violation of Christian law and ceremony.

> As the destiny of the day falls out, my lord,
> [explains Gnotho,] one goes out to wedding,
> another goes to hanging. And your grace, in
> the due consideration, shalt find 'em much
> alike; the one hath the ring upon her finger,
> the other a halter about her neck. "I take

44 In Ben Jonson's *Neptune's Triumph for the Return to
Albion* (1624), for example, the antimasque of sailors appears just before the last song and the final dance of the
performance.

thee Beatrice," says the bridegroom. "I take
thee Agatha," says the hangman; and both say
together, "To have to to hold 'til death do
part us."

(V.i.442-9)

The irony inherent within the women's names would not be
missed. Siren, only this once given the name of Beatrice,
is to be elevated as was her chaste namesake whereas Agatha,
as was hers, is to be martyred. Nor, indeed, would the
blasphemous mockery of the marriage ritual go unnoticed.
Bragging then compounds Gnotho's insolence as he proceeds to
link his obedience to secular law with that of Holy Writ.
As a "dutiful subject and obedient to the law" (V.i.452), he
claims to have but shown himself as having more foresight
than other men. Besides, he protests with fine irony, "The
clerk shall take his oath and the church book shall be sworn
too" (V.i.449-501).

When it finally sinks in on the enterprising clown that
Evander's original edict has, indeed, been rescinded,
Gnotho's wedding music turns to comic lament:

Oh music! No music, but prove most doleful
trumpets;
Oh bride! No bride, but thou mayst prove a
strumpet;
Oh venture! No venture, I have for one now
none;
Oh wife! Thy life is sav'd when I hoped it
had been gone.
Case up your fruitless string! No penny,
no wedding;
Case up thy maidenhead! No priest, no bedding,
Avaunt my venture, it can ne'er be restored,
'Til Ag, my old wife, be thrown overboard.
Then, come again, old Ag, since it must be so,
Let bride and venture with woeful music go.

(V.i.559-568)

Like Hieronimo, whose tragic lines he parodies, he too
looks forward to what seems to him a "lively form of
death."[45] Tearfully and with his usual lack of decorum, the

---

[45] Thomas Kyd, *The Spanish Tragedy* III.ii.1 ff.

clown honours Evander for his kindness and then advises
him, "Heaven bless and mend your laws that they do not gull
your poor countrymen [in this] fashion. But I am not the
first by forty that has been undone by the law" (V.i.595-7).
These final words, of course, keep Gnotho sqaurely within
the thematic structure of the play as it comes to its close.
"All hopes dashed," he sadly leaves the stage followed
shortly after by the servants whose "ventures" also failed.
With the withdrawal of what have been seen here as antimasque figures the final masque unions can take place.
Penitent sons are rejoined to restored fathers; "tears of
faith in woman's breast" confirm a "happy renovation" between husband and erring wife; and "devoted knees" bend to
"age-honoured shrine[s]" (V.i.646-51). With a final proclamation by Evander which is tantamount to a call to
revels:

> Let music be the crown
> And set this high: "The good needs fear no law,
> It is his safety, and the bad man's awe,"

> (V.i.698-700)

the company sweeps off stage to the accompaniment of a
flourish of horns and trumpets.

Only about five hundred lines of *The Old Law* are given
over exclusively to Gnotho and the farcical level of the
play. Another one hundred seventy lines, in which he
provides the antimasque juxtaposition within a traditional
comic conclusion, still amount to less than one quarter of
the play. Yet, quite obviously, his brief appearances suc-
cussfully carry the third and lowest level of the drama and
serve, ironically, to point up, either through farcical
parallel or contrast, the action and the moral issues of the
main plots. In addition, they are a credit to William
Rowley's skill as a collaborator by virtue of their fine
integration into the play, both structurally and thematically,
and as a writer of genuine humour in the vein of farcical
comedy. If there is a shadow of cynicism cast over *The Old
Law* and, in particular, over its rather simplistic conclusion, it is cast by Middleton's attitude to humanity
rather than by Rowley's. With Rowley there is an open-eyed
acceptance of the tendency of man to use circumstances to
his own advantage and a sense of naive glee in the simple
determination that right and morality will ultimately pre-

vail. That Gnotho exits resigned rather than reformed
bothers him not a whit and it does not bother the audience
either. The words of the theatre critic John Mason Brown
apply as much to Jacobean farce as to modern. "The sole
point and justification of a farce is that it be funny. It
is a comedy written with a slapstick rather than a pen. Its
business is to make us accept the impossible as possible,
the deranged as normal, and silliness as a happy substitute
for sense." As such, farce depends in technique upon
rapid stage action, specific verbal references caught
quickly by the ear (often topical or at least contemporary),
bawdy horseplay, and visual metaphor which, though perhaps
lacking in subtlety, evokes instant audience response.
Sustained or extended patterns of verbal metaphor depending
upon abstract or philosophic comprehension are practically
non-existent.

        This is, of course, not so in the serious level of *The
Old Law*. The Cleanthes-Hippolita-Leonides sequences and
those which involve Simonides in their fate have little
actual stage action. They are, however, permeated with
central and controlling verbal metaphoric patterns, the
principal of which play the changes on the dichotomy between what is *natural* and *unnatural*, upon the distinction
between *fortune* and *nature*, and upon the subtlety inherent
within definitions of *nature* itself. The difference, for
example, between impartial and benevolent nature is established very early in the play. When Cleanthes makes his
first entrance, Simonides greets him:

            Oh lad, here's a spring for young plants to
                                    flourish!
            The old trees must down [that] kept the sun
                                    from us;
            We shall rise now, boy.

The ensuing rejoinders make clear the differences in attitude:

            CLEANTHES Whither, sir, I pray?
              To the bleak air of storms, among those trees
              Which we had shelter from?

            SIMONIDES Yes, from our growth,

    The Saturday Review of Literature, XXXIV (March 24,
1951), 26.

                Our sap, and livelihood, and from our fruit!

                                          (I.i.80-7)

Simonides is identified with impartial nature in which
"vegetives" take advantage of the cycle of youth and age,
life and death, to advance their fortune. Cleanthes, on
the other hand, is identified with benevolent nature which
sees maturity and age as the protecting parents of grateful
youth. The lawyers defend the new edict on the ground that
it is an ally to nature. By cutting off the aged "as
fruitless to the republic," the "law shall finish what
nature lingered at" (I.i.122-3). In fact, the edict itself
refers to the aged as being "in their decayed nature" (I.i.
147-8). In opposition to such legal sophistry which speaks
of assisting nature in pruning the state of near-dead wood,
old Creon reminds his listeners that life is not one cycle
but a series.

          I have felt [, he says,] nature's winter
                                    sicknesses,
          Yet ever kept a lively sap in me
          To greet the cheerful spring of health again.

                                          (I.i.246-8)

With great spirit he refuses to "blame time, nature, nor my
stars" (I.i.254) and places the full responsibility for his
death on tyranny. Creon insists that the new edict seeks
to take from nature a decision which is inherently hers -
to decide a life span. Nature, he insists, will retaliate
by extending life as long as she can..
     Cleanthes recognizes both these aspects of nature when
he questions:

          Does the kind root bleed out his livelihood
          In parent distribution to his branches,
          Adorning them with all his glorious fruits,
          Proud that his pride is seen when he's unseen?
          And must not gratitude descend again
          To comfort his old limbs in fruitless winter?

                                          (I.i.345-50)

                          xlv

Accepting that there is both the nature which is an impartial life force and that there is a nobility of which human nature, by virtue of its capacity for pity and compassion, is capable, he then prays:

> Improvident, or at least partial Nature,
> Weak woman in this kind, who in thy last
> Teeming still forgets the former, ever making
> The burden of thy last throes the dearest
> Darling; oh yet in noble man reform it,
> And make us better than those vegetives
> Whose souls die within 'em. Nature, as thou
> art old,
> If love and justice be not dead in thee,
> Make some the pattern of thy piety
> Lest all do turn unnaturally against thee,
> And thou be blamed for our oblivions
> And brutish reluctation!

(I.i.351-62)

Whole nature is thus both "vegetive" and moral; whereas survival-of-the-fittest nature is "partial" in that it rejects those enlightened beings who also come under the laws of moral governance. Secular law, as represented in Evander's edict, has allied itself with "partial" nature - it is *un*wholesome as are those who pursue its advantage. The *whole*some has been seen throughout Act I in the relationships between Cleanthes, Hippolita, and Leonides and the link between secular law and nature visualized in the unity of Cleanthes and Hippolita in Holy Matrimony and as they are *natural* son and daughter-in-*law* to Leonides. As for the court of Epire itself, Hippolita makes it very clear when she tries to convince Leonides to flee the state, that when a mother, in this case Epire, becomes "unnatural" then a "stepmother" is to be preferred (I.i.445-6). The wooded area in which Leonides is secreted apart from the court is described as being framed by "provident heavens" (I.i.482); a place where the "air's much wholesomer" (IV.i.31). Evander, while still playing the part of the originator and supporter of the Old Law, declares his "court looks like a spring" after the "old weeds [the aged men and women] are gone" (II.i.38-9); whereas it is clear that the court is overrun with parasites. When, in the last act, Evander exposes his hoax, he uses the same image pattern. He has desired, he says, to see "the flowers and weeds that grew

about our court" (V.i.689) and in the restoration of moral
order it is the weeds that are pruned back and the flowers
which are allowed to flourish.

The comic level of representation of *The Old Law*, those
scenes which involve Simonides, Eugenia, and Lisander, com-
bines the dramatic methods of each of the other levels. In
terms of metaphoric technique the comic level comes, as it
were, between the two representations which flank it; it
employs both the contemplative and predominantly verbal
method of the serious and the spontaneous and predominantly
visual method of the farce. After Simonides is established
as the disloyal son and Eugenia as the disloyal wife, their
machinations proceed, action after action, to support this
characterization. As opposed to Cleanthes and Hippolita,
they are "partial" nature, more concerned with fortune and
self-advancement than with love and justice. Even when
faced with the touching fidelity of his parents, Simonides
has the effrontery to suggest that Antigona can live out
her remaining years in the enjoyment of a young courtier.
To this Antigona turns on him with the name "unnatural."
Completely unabashed, his response indicates his contempt
for morality:

> Then I am no fool I'm sure,
> For to be natural at such a time
> Were a fool's part indeed.

(II.i.121-5)

Eugenia's concept of nature as exclusively physical parallels his attitude, as does her brazenness. When Parthenia,
Lisander's daughter, implies criticism of the "feathered
fools" that dare to court Eugenia while Lisander lives,
the stepmother advises her:

> . . . always take age first to make thee rich;
> That was my counsel ever, and then youth
> Will make thee sport enough all thy life after.

(II.ii.139-41)

For both of these "unnaturals" the weeds of wealth and
sexuality have overgrown morality.

In metaphoric terms, however, it is the actions of
Lisander which most clearly provide an interchange with the

xlvii

verbal and visual patternings of the play. Lisander tries
to deceive secular law by deceiving natural law; he tries
to avoid the penalty of Evander's edict by avoiding the
cycle of human mortality. Before the audience's eyes,
Lisander

> Takes counsel with the secrets of all art
> To make himself youthful again.

> > (III.ii.19-20)

The old man is at once laughable and pathetic. He is no
more capable of performing "horsetricks" than "whores'
tricks." Although natural indignation heats his temper to
the point where he challenges and defeats Simonides and his
crew in a mock tourney of dancing, fencing, and drinking,
he is himself attempting the unnatural. As Cleanthes
questions him:

> Would you begin to work ne'er yet attempted,
> To pull time backward?

> > (III.ii.258-9)

Earlier Lisander had branded the forward young courtiers
as "shames of nature" and "monsters unnatural," (II.ii.81-3).
Now, ironically, Cleanthes accuses Lisander of being "more
than shameful" (III.ii.242), of changing the "livery of
saints and angels / For this mixed monstrousness!" (III.ii.
252-3). All laughter is dispelled as Cleanthes insists that
such forcing of "ground / That has been so long hallowed
like a temple, / To bring forth fruits of earth now" (III.
ii.253-5) is a defilement of both natural and moral order.

> . . . . For what is age [, he argues,]
> But the holy place of life, chapel of ease
> For all men's wearied miseries; and, to rob
> That of her ornament, it is accursed,
> As from a priest to steal a holy vestment;
> Aye, and convert it to a sinful covering.

> > (III.ii.279-84)

The hilarity of visual impact gained by seeing the old dog
actually attempting new tricks which are unnatural to its

age is thus combined through the extension of verbal
metaphor with the seriousness of the moral implications of
Lisander's actions which at once attempt to violate the
sanctity of age and to deny the natural order of life.
Such actions are tantamount to blasphemy in that they
transgress the laws of nature, both "vegetive" and noble,
and those of divine governance.

Although it is obvious that old Lisander has learned
his lesson at the end of the play, questions can certainly
be raised about Eugenia and Simonides. Lisander says:

> If there be tears of faith in woman's breast,
> I have received a myriad which confirms me
> To find a happy renovation,

(V.i.648-50)

and from this we can assume Eugenia at least *shows* repentance even though she says not a word. In fact, her
last words in the play only express her refusal to be
judged by Hippolita (V.i.384). As for Simonides, he too
can put on a show. With the other courtiers, he falls on
his knees before the aged fathers and pours forth "salt
sorrow" (V.i.624, 631-2) but he does so, as he admits,
because "there's no remedy" (V.i.631-2) for the situation in
which he finds himself. His last words are a sardonic pun.
To Evander's declaration, "We have now seen / The flowers
and weeds that grew about our court," he glances down at
the ornate clothing which his ill-gotten wealth has provided and mutters, "If these be weeds, I'm afraid I shall
wear none so good again as long as my father lives" (V.i.
713-14). *The Old Law* ends then realistically rather than
romantically. For Middleton and Rowley weeds such as
Simonides and Eugenia and, of course, Gnotho, do not *become*
flowers. They can only be contained by just and loving
gardeners. Epire does not *become* Eden. Rather it achieves
a condition which is the best that man in his postlapsarian
state can provide.

NOTE ON THE TEXT

The only early edition of *The Old Law* is a deplorably
bad quarto printed for the London book-seller Edward Archer
in 1656. George R. Price presents evidence to support his
conjectures that the state of the first edition was the
result of a series of circumstances each of which subjected
the text to additions, deletions, misinterpretations, and
misreadings.[47] The first state, the Middleton-Rowley collaboration, appears to have been a prompt-copy (perhaps in
part in Rowley's own hand) which included some few stage
directions but a number of anticipatory warnings by which
the book-holder could cue actors to prepare for entrances
and musicians for some instrumental accompaniment. Lacking
were directions necessary for readers only, such as asides.
This prompt-copy was then re-written, at least in part, by
Massinger at which time he made some textual revisions and
expansions possible to be included in a later performance.
Ultimately, when the manuscript came into the hands of
Edward Archer, either he or one of his editors proceeded
to make further changes in preparation for publication.
Finally, the manuscript was turned over to compositors (the
difference in kind and number of errors in various parts of
the text indicate more than one) who were then responsible
for setting the type. The result of this progression is
the hodge-podge bad quarto of 1656 in which the *dramatis
personae* indicates family relationships which do not exist,
anticipatory cues appear as speech headings, directions to
musicians and property men are included as part of the
dialogue, to say nothing of numererous textual absurdities
resulting from misreadings.

The only thing that can be said for the quarto is that
once the compositors had added their errors to what must
have already been a corrupt manuscript, they made but one
change. In the collation of eight copies of the quarto
(BM1 [the Ashley Library copy which was used as control
text], BM2, BM3, BM4, Folger, Huntington, Newberry, Stark)
only one textual variant was found. On D1v (II.i.107),
those copies obviously earlier in the run (BM3, BM4, Folger,
and Stark), the word *prepartion* appears; in the later im-
pressions the printer has corrected this to *preparation*
(Ashley, BM2, Huntington, and Newberry).

The text with the fly-leaf and title-page, half-sheets

47 *op. cit.* pp. 117-25

1

which are conjugate to L1 and L2 at the end of the play
proper, was assembled independently from the catalogue of
plays appended to *The Old Law* when it was bound for sale.
The catalogue is separately paginated, (a1) through (b4),
and, judging from a cursory examination of type, may even
have been printed in a different shop. Greg points out that
Archer was housed at the Adam and Eve whereas George Pollard,
another dealer, owned the Ben Jonson's Head. Pollard's
later associations with Francis Kirkham, the noted play
collector who was responsible for the 1661 and 1671 catalogues suggest to Greg the possibility that Pollard and not
Archer was responsible for compiling what we now call the
Archer catalogue (III, 1328). This suggestion would account
for Pollard's shop being included in the introduction to the
catalogue whereas it is not mentioned on the title-page.
Thus, the fact that Jane Bell's device appears at the end
of the catalogue indicates only that she was responsible for
printing the catalogue, not necessarily the whole quarto as
George R. Price claims.[48]

Whether all copies of the 1656 quarto included the
catalogue is impossible to tell. Of those examined, four
have it (Ashley, BM2, Folger, Huntington); whereas the
other four are lacking. They may, however, have had the
catalogue originally but have subsequently lost it.

For this text, all of the modern editions have been
consulted and many obvious textual emendations accepted without comment. All substantial variants have been noted.
Every effort has been made to adhere to the quarto text
wherever possible. All editorial emendations have been
acknowledged in the glossary at the bottom of each page.
Asterisks in the dialogue indicate that explanatory notes
are provided at the back of the text (pp. 124-36).

[48] *ibid.* p. 118.

MODERN EDITIONS

Modern reprints of *The Old Law* have been included in the following collections. Each has been consulted for this edition.

The Works of Philip Massinger, ed. Thomas Coexter (London, 1759), vol IV.

The Dramatic Works of Philip Massinger, ed. John Monck Mason (London, 1779), vol. IV.

The Plays of Philip Massinger, ed. William Gifford (London, 1805), vol. IV.

The Dramatic Works of Massinger and Ford, with introduction by Hartley Coleridge (London, 1840).

The Works of Thomas Middleton, ed. Alexander Dyce (London, 1840), vol. I.

The Works of Thomas Middleton, ed. A. H. Bullen (London, 1885), vol. II.

SUGGESTED READING

Asp, Carolyn. *A Study of Thomas Middleton's Tragicomedies,* Jacobean Drama Studies 28 (Salzburg, 1974).

Bald, R. C. "The Chronology of Middleton's Plays," *MLR,* XXXII (1937), 33-43.

Barker, R. H. *Thomas Middleton* (New York, 1958).

Bullock, Helene. "Thomas Middleton and the Fashion in Playmaking," *PMLA,* XLII (1927), 766-76.

Eccles, Mark. "Middleton's Birth and Education," *RES,* VII (1931), 431-41.

Hildebrand, Harold N. "Thomas Middleton's *The Viper's Brood,*" *MLN,* XLII (1927),35-8.

Holmes, David M. *The Art of Thomas Middleton: A Critical Study* (Oxford, 1970).

Maxwell, Baldwin. *Studies in Beaumont, Fletcher, and Massinger* (Chapel Hill, 1939).

Morris, E. C. "On the Date and Composition of *The Old Law,*" *PMLA,* XVII (1902), 1-70.

Phialas, P. G. "Middleton's Early Contact with the Law," *SP,* LII (1955) 186-94.

Price, George R. "The Authorship and the Manuscript of *The Old Law,*" *HLQ,* XVI (1953), 117-39.

Robb, Dewar M. "The Canon of William Rowley's Plays," *MLR,* XLV (1950), 129-41.

Schoenbaum, Samuel, "Middleton's Tragicomedies," *MP,* LIV (1956-7), 7-19.

Stork, Charles Wharton. *William Rowley: His "All's Lost by Lust," and "A Shoemaker, A Gentleman," with an Introduction on Rowley's Place in the Drama* (Philadelphia, 1910).

Wiggins, Pauline G. *An Inquiry into the Authorship of the Middleton-Rowley Plays* (Boston, 1897).

THE

Excellent *Comedy, called*

THE OLD LAW:

A new way to pleafe you.

By
{ *Phil. Maſſinger.*
{ *Tho. Middleton.*
{ *William Rowley.*

Acted before the King and Queene at *Salisbury House,*
and at severall other places, with great Applaufe.

Together with an exact and perfect Catalogue of all
the Playes, with the Authors Names, and what are
Comedies, Tragedies, Hiftories, Paftoralls,
Masks, Interludes, more exactly Printed
then ever before.

LONDON,
Printed for *Edward Archer*, at the figne of the *Adam*
and *Eve*, in *Little Britaine*. 1656.

Title page of the 1656 Quarto of *The Old Law.*

1

PERSONS OF THE PLAY

EVANDER, DUKE *of* EPIRE
CREON, *father to* SIMONIDES
LEONIDES, *father to* CLEANTHES
SIMONIDES
   young courtiers
CLEANTHES
LISANDER, *uncle to* CLEANTHES
GNOTHO, *the clown*
CRATILUS, *the executioner*
CREON'S *servants*
  Butler
  Bailiff
  Tailor
  Cook
  Footman
  Coachman
[*Dancing Master*]
Parish Clerk
Drawer
Courtiers
Lawyers
[*Fiddlers, Officers, Servants, etc.*]
ANTIGONA, *wife to* CREON, *mother to* SIMONIDES
HIPPOLITA, *wife to* CLEANTHES
EUGENIA, *wife to* LISANDER
PARTHENIA, *daughter to* LISANDER
AGATHA, *wife to* GNOTHO
SIREN, *a wench*
[*Old women, wives to* CREON'S *servants*]

     Scene: EPIRE

2

THE OLD LAW

Act I, scene i

Enter SIMONIDES *and two lawyers*

SIMONIDES   Is the law firm, sir?

1 LAWYER   The law! What more firm, sir,
More powerful, forcible, or more permanent?

SIMONIDES   By my troth, sir,
I partly do believe it. Conceive, sir,   5
You have [but] indirectly answered my question;
I did not doubt the fundamental grounds
Of law in general for the most solid,
But this particular law that me concerns
Now, at the present, if that be firm and strong   10
And powerful, and forcible, and permanent?
I am a young man that has an old father.

2 LAWYER   Nothing more strong, sir,
It is *Secundum statutum principis*
Confirmatum cum voce senatus,   15
Et voce reipublicae, nay *consummatum*
Et exemplificatum. Is it not in force
When diverse have already tasted it
And paid their lives for penalty?

SIMONIDES   'Tis true.   20
My father must be next; this day completes
Full fourscore years upon him.

2 LAWYER   He's here then,
Sub poena statuti; hence, I can tell him
Truer than all the physicians in the world,   25
He cannot live out tomorrow. This is
The most certain climacterical year;

5 *conceive* consider, understand
14-17 *Secundum statutum principis Confirmatum cum voce sena-*
tus (senatum Q)*Et voce reipublicae* (republica Q), nay *con-*
summatum et exemplificatum. 'According to the Prince's
statutes.'
18 *diverse* various persons
24 *Sub poena statuti* 'according to the penalty of the law'

'Tis past all danger, for there's no 'scaping it.
What age is your mother, sir?

SIMONIDES   Faith, near her days too;   30
Wants some two of three score.*

1 LAWYER   So! She'll drop away
One of these days too. Here's a good age now
For those that have old parents and rich inheritance!

SIMONIDES   And, sir, 'tis profitable for others too: 35
Are there not fellows that lie bed-rid in their offices
That younger men would walk lustily in?
Churchmen, that even the second infancy
Hath silenced, yet have spun out their lives so long
That many pregnant and ingenious spirits   40
Have languished in their hoped reversions,
And died upon the thought? And, by your leave, sir,
Have you not places filled up in the law
By some grave senators that you imagine
Have held them long enough, and such spirits as you,   45
Were they removed, would leap into their dignities?

1 LAWYER   *Dic quibus in terris, et eris mihi magnus Apollo.*

SIMONIDES   But tell me, faith, your fair opinion:
Is it not a sound and necessary law,
This by the Duke enacted?   50

1 LAWYER   Never did Greece,
Our ancient seat of brave philosophers,
'Mongst all her *nomothetae* and lawgivers,

27 *climacterical* a period in human life when a change
occurs
28 *danger* power to dispose of (*Obs*. OED)
31 Astericks indicate explanatory notes are to be found at
the back of the text
38 *the second infancy* senility   *have* ed. (hath Q)
40 *pregnant* prolific, teeming
40 *ingenious* having genius (*Obs*. OED)
46 *dignities* high positions
47 *dic quibus in terris, et eris mihi magnus Apollo*. 'Tell
me in what ground and thou shalt be Apollo great to me'.
Virgil, *The Bucoliks . . . Together with his Georgiks*, All
newly translated into English by A.F. Abraham Fleming ,
London, 1589, iii, 19 ClV).
53 *nomothetae* ed. (nomotheta Q) a general word for 'law-

Not when she flourished in her sevenfold sages*
Whose living memory can never die,   55
Produce a law more grave and necessary.

SIMONIDES   I'm of that mind too.

2 LAWYER   I will maintain, sir,
Draco's* oligarchy, that the government
Of community reduced into few,   60
Framed a fair state; Solon's* *chreokopia*,
That cut off poor men's debts to their rich creditors,
Was good and charitable, but not full allowed;
His *seisactheia* did reform that error,
His honourable senate of Areopagitae.*   65
Lycurgus* was more loose and gave too free
And licentious reins unto his discipline -
As that a young woman, in her husband's weakness,
Might choose her able friend to propagate,
That so the commonwealth might be supplied   70
With hope of lusty spirits. Plato* did err,
And so did Aristotle,* allowing
Lewd and luxurious limits to their laws.
But now our Epire, our Epire's Evander,
Our noble and wise Prince, has hit the law   75
That all our predecesive students
Have missed, unto their shame. *Enter* CLEANTHES

SIMONIDES   Forbear the praise, sir,

makers but in Athens it was used especially for a commit-
tee to draft or revise laws (OED)
59 *oligarchy* government by the few
59-60 *government of community* the commonwealth
61 *fram'd* fashioned
61 *chreokopia* ed. (creocopedi Q) 'a cancelling of all
debts' (OCD)
63 *full allowed* fully accepted as satisfactory (*Obs*. OED)
64 *seisactheia* ed. (sisaithie Q) literally 'the shaking off
of burdens.' The measures adopted by Solon (see above 1.61)
which included the cancelling of debt and the forbidding of
borrowed using the person as security (OCD).
67 *licentious* morally unrestrained
68 *As that* for example
73 *luxurious* unrestrained
76 *predecesive* those who have gone before; preceding (*Obs*.
only example cited in OED)

'Tis in itself most pleasing. Cleanthes!
Oh lad, here's a spring for young plants to flourish! 80
The old trees must down [that] kept the sun from us;
We shall rise now, boy.

CLEANTHES Whither, sir, I pray?
To the bleak air of storms, among those trees
Which we had shelter from?   85

SIMONIDES   Yes, from our growth,
Our sap, and livelihood, and from our fruit!
What? 'Tis not jubilee with thee yet, I think,
Thou lookst so sad on it. How old's thy father?

CLEANTHES
Jubilee! No, indeed, 'tis a bad year with me.   90

SIMONIDES
Prithee, how old's thy father? Then, I can tell thee.

CLEANTHES   I know not how to answer you, Simonides.
He's too old, being now exposed
Unto the rigour of a cruel edict,
And yet not old enough by many years,   95
'Cause I'd not see him go an hour before me.

SIMONIDES   These very passions I speak to my father.
Come, come, here's none but friends here, we may speak
Our insides freely; these are lawyers, man,
And shall be counsellors shortly.   100

CLEANTHES   They shall be now, sir,
And shall have large fees if they'll undertake
To help a good cause for it wants assistance;
Bad ones, I know, they can insist upon.

1 LAWYER   Oh, sir, we must undertake of both parts, 105

80 *spring* a supply of water
88 *jubilee* a time for celebration
94 *rigour* strict terms (see 1610 Heywood *The Golden Age*
[B3ᵛ] One lovely boy / Hath felt the rigor of that strict
decree.)
97 *passions* extravagant emotions
99 *insides* innermost thoughts
103 *assistance* support

But the good we have most good in.

CLEANTHES   Pray you, say,
How do you allow of this strange edict?

1 LAWYER   *Secundum justitiam,* by my faith, sir,
The happiest edict that ever was in Epire.   110

CLEANTHES   What, to kill innocents, sir? It cannot be;
It is no rule in justice there to punish.*

1 LAWYER   Oh, sir,
You understand a conscience, but not law.

CLEANTHES   Why, sir, is there so main a difference?   115

1 LAWYER   [*Laughing*]
You'll never be [a] good lawyer if you understand not that.

CLEANTHES   I think then 'tis the best to be a bad one.

1 LAWYER   Why, sir, the very letter and the sense
Do both o'erthrow you in this statute,
Which speaks: that every man living to   120
Fourscore years, and women to threescore, shall then
Be cut off as fruitless to the republic,
And law shall finish what nature lingered at.

CLEANTHES   And this suit shall soon be dispatched in law?

1 LAWYER   It is so plain it can have no demur,   125
The church-book overthrows it.

CLEANTHES   And so it does,

106 *But the . . . good in.* 'The best are those we can make
most money from.'
109 *Secundum justitiam* 'according to the law'
112 *It is no rule . . . to punish.* 'The law cannot be just
if it punishes the innocent.'
118 *sense* ed. (sense both Q)
119 *o'erthrow you* deny your position
120 *Which speaks* ed. (Which that speaks Q)
125 *It can have no demur* 'There can be no objections'
126 *church-book* church register of births
126 *overthrows* has authority over (see above l. 119)

The church-book overthrows it if you read it well.

1 LAWYER   Still you run from the law into error!
You say it takes the lives of innocents;   130
I say no, and so says common reason.
What man lives to fourscore and woman to three
That can die innocent?

CLEANTHES   A fine lawful evasion!
Good sir, rehearse the full statute to me.   135

SIMONIDES   Fie! That's too tedious, you have already
The full sum in the brief relation.

CLEANTHES   Sir,
'Mongst many words may be found contradictions,
And these men dare sue and wrangle with a statute,   140
If they can pick a quarrel with some error.

2 LAWYER *[Draws forth statute]*
Listen, sir, I'll gather it as brief as I can for you:
*[Reads] Anno primo Evandri, be it for the care and good
of the commonwealth, for diverse necessary reasons that
we shall urge, thus peremptorily enacted:* -   145

CLEANTHES   A fair pretence, if the reasons foul it not!

2 LAWYER
*That all men living in our dominions of Epire in their
decayed nature to the age of fourscore, or women to the
age of threescore, shall on the same day be instantly
put to death, by those means and instruments that a*   150

128 *church-book* the Bible, Holy Writ (see above 1. 126)
128 *overthrows* upsets, destroys (see above 1. 126)
135 *rehearse* read over
137 *The full sum* the substance of the meaning
140 *sue and wrangle* argue and dispute.
142 *gather it* bring it together.
143 *Anno primo Evandri* 'in the first year [of the reign of]
Evander'
145 *peremptorily* decisively, precluding debate.
146 *A fair . . . foul it not!* 'A plausible claim to merit, if
the purposes for deviating from strict justice (OED 5b) are
not criminally implicated' (*Obs.* OED 7b).
148 *decayed nature* old age.

former proclamation had to this purpose, through our
said territories dispersed.

CLEANTHES   There was no woman in this senate, certain.

2 LAWYER
That these men, being past their bearing arms to aid and
defend their country, past their manhood and livelihood
to propogate any further issue to their posterity, and,
as well, past their counsels (which overgrown gravity is
now run into dotage) to assist their country; to whom,
in common reason, nothing should be so wearisome as their
own lives; as, it may be supposed, [they are] tedious to
their successive heirs whose times are spent in the good
of their country, yet, wanting the means to maintain it,
are like to grow old before their inheritance born to
them come to their necessary use, [and they be condemned
to death.] For the women, for that they were never   165
defence to their country, never by counsel admitted to
the assist of government of their country, only necessary
to the propagation of posterity, and, now, at the age of
threescore, be past that good and all their goodness; it
is thought fit, then, a quarter abated from the more   170
worthy member, they be put to death as is before recited.
For the just and impartial execution of this our statute,
the example shall first begin in and about our court,
which ourself will see carefully performed, and not for a
full month following extend any further into our   175
dominions. Dated the sixth of the second month at our
Palace Royal in Epire.

CLEANTHES   A fine edict, and very fairly gilded!
And is there no scruple in all these words

154-177 This is a very confusing passage syntactically. The
sense of the meaning has been attempted here with as little
change in the Quarto text as possible.
157 *counsels* power to advise
157 *overgrown gravity* excessive seriousness
158 *dotage* senility.
160 [*they are*] *tedious* ed. (is tedious Q)
165 *For the women* ed.(and are like Q)
169 *be past* ed. (to be past Q)
170 *abated* subtracted
171 *they be* ed. (to be Q)
172 *For the* ed. (provided that for the Q)
178 *gilded* ornamented with words

To demur the law upon occasion?   180

SIMONIDES   Pox, 'tis an unnecessary inquisition!
Prithee, set him not about it.

2 LAWYER   Troth, none, sir.
It is so evident and plain a case
There is no succour for the defendant.   185

CLEANTHES   Possible can nothing help in a good case?

1 LAWYER   Faith, sir, I do think there may be a hole
Which would protract delay, if not remedy.

CLEANTHES
Why, there's some comfort in that. Good sir, speak it.

1 LAWYER   Nay, you must pardon me for that, sir.   190

SIMONIDES   Prithee, do not;
It may ope[n] a wound to many sons and heirs
That may die after it.

CLEANTHES [*Taking out his purse*]
Come, sir, I know
How to make you speak. Will this do it? [*Gives him money*]

1 LAWYER   I will afford you my opinion sir.

CLEANTHES   Pray you, repeat the literal words, expressly
The time of death.

180 *To demur* to delay; to suspend action.
181 *Pox* an exclamation of impatience (*Obs.* OED) having its
source in plague references, ie., "a pox on him" and "a
plague on both your houses" (*All's Well* IV.iii. 307; *R.J.*
III.i.94).
181 *inquisition* questioning
185 *succour* refuge
188 *protract delay* to extend time so as to cause delay
192-3 *It may ope[n]. . . after it.* 'Many who stand to
profit by the law as it stands, may lose their expectations
if a loop-hole if found.'
196 *afford* Pun; yield (OED 5); manage to sell (*Obs.* OED 4b)
197 *expressly* particularly, specifically

SIMONIDES
  'Tis an unnecessary question; prithee, let it alone.

2 LAWYER   Hear his opinion; 'twill be fruitless, sir. 200
  [Reading again] That men at the age of fourscore and
  women at threescore, shall the same day be put to death.

1 LAWYER   Thus I help the man to twenty-one years more.

CLEANTHES   That were a fair addition.

1 LAWYER   Mark it, sir, we say man is not at age   205
  Till he be one-and-twenty; before, 'tis infancy
  And adolescency. Now, by that addition,
  Fourscore he cannot be till a hundred and one.

SIMONIDES   Oh, poor evasion!
  He's fourscore years old, sir.   210

1 LAWYER   That helps more, sir.
  He begins to be old at fifty; so, at fourscore,
  He's but thirty years old. So, believe it, sir,
  He may be twenty years in declination,
  And so long may a man linger and live by it.   215

SIMONIDES   The worst hope of safety that e'er I heard!
  Give him his fee again, 'tis not worth two dinars.

1 LAWYER   There's no law for restitution of fees, sir.

CLEANTHES
  No, no, sir, I meant it lost when 'twas given.

SIMONIDES *[To the Lawyers]*   *Enter* CREON *and* ANTIGONA
  No more, good sir,   220
  Here are ears unnecessary for your doctrine.

199 *prithee* I pray thee
201 *men* ed. (man Q)
206 *'tis* ed. (his Q)
207 *Now* ed. (nor Q)
214 *declination* a gradual falling off from vigour
217 *dinars* "The dinar[r] is gold worth thirty shillings,"
(Sir Thomas Herbert, *Some Years Travels* . . . [2nd ed.
London, 1638], p. 38).
219 *No, no* . . . *'twas given* 'I never expected to receive
any refund.'

1 LAWYER   I have spoke out my fee and I have done, sir.

SIMONIDES   Oh, my dear father!

CREON   Tush! Meet me not in exclaims;
    I understand the worst and hope no better.   225
    A fine law! If this hold, white heads will be cheap
    And many watchmen's places will be vacant;
    Forty of 'em I know my seniors,
    That did due deeds of darkness too. Their country
    Has watched 'em a good turn for it and ta'en 'em   230
    Napping now.* The fewer hospitals will serve, too;
    Many may be used for stews and brothels,
    And those people will never trouble 'em to fourscore.

ANTIGONA   Can you play and sport with sorrow, sir?

CREON   Sorrow for what, Antigona? For my life?   235
    My sorrow is, I have kept it so long well
    With bringing it up unto so ill an end.
    I might have gently lost it in my cradle,
    Before my nerves and ligaments grew strong
    To bind it faster to me.   240

SIMONIDES   For mine own sake
    I should have been sorry for that.

CREON   In my youth
    I was a soldier, no coward in my age,
    I never turned my back upon my foe;   245
    I have felt nature's winter sicknesses,*
    Yet ever kept a lively sap in me
    To greet the cheerful spring of health again.
    Dangers on horseback, on foot, by water,
    I have 'scaped to this day; and yet this day,   250
    Without all help of casual accidents,
    Is only deadly to me 'cause it numbers

224 *exclaims* outcries
227 *watchmen's* guardians'
232 *stews and brothels* whore houses
233 *those people* the inmates of "stews and brothels,"
prostitutes
236 *My sorrow is* ed. (My sorrows Q)
247 *a lively sap* a quickened blood
251 *casual* unexpected

Fourscore years to me. Where's the fault now?
I cannot blame time, nature, nor my stars,
Nor aught but tyranny. Even kings themselves   255
Have sometimes tasted an even fate with me.
He that has been a soldier all his days,
And stood in personal opposition
'Gainst darts and arrows, extremes of heat,
And pinching cold, has treacherously at home   260
In his secured quiet, by a villain's hand
Been basely lost in his star's ignorance;
And so must I die by a tyrant's sword.

1 LAWYER   Oh, say not so, sir, it is by the law!

CREON
  And what's that, sir, but the sword of tyranny   265
When it is brandished against innocent lives?
I'm now upon my death bed, sir, and 'tis fit
I should unbosom my free conscience,
And show the faith I die in. I do believe
'Tis tyranny that takes my life.   270

SIMONIDES [*Aside*]
  Would it were gone
By one means or [an]other. What a long day
Will this be ere night.

CREON   Simonides.

SIMONIDES   Here [I] sit, weeping.   275

CREON   Wherefore dost thou weep?

CLEANTHES [*Aside*]
  'Cause you make no more haste to your end.

253 *Where's . . . now?* 'Where, then does the error lie?'
255 *nor aught* nothing
256 *even* same
261 *secured* free from fear or anxiety
261 *Been* ed. (Am Q)
262 *his* ed. (my Q)
268 *I should . . . conscience* 'I should express my own
conviction.'
275 *Here [I] sit, weeping.* ed. (Heer sit_____ _____
weeping. Q) Another possibility is to relegate *weeping*
to a stage direction.

SIMONIDES   How can you question nature so unjustly?
  I had a grandfather, and then had not you
  True filial tears for him?   280

CLEANTHES   [*Aside*] Hypocrite!
  A disease of drought dry up all pity from him
  That can dissemble pity with wet eyes.

CREON   Be good unto your mother, Simonides,
  She must be now your care.   285

ANTIGONA   To what end, sir?
  The bell of this sharp edict tolls for me
  As it rings out for you. I'll be as ready,
  With one hour's stay, to go along with you.

CREON   Thou must not, woman. There are years behind 290
  Before thou canst set forward in this voyage,
  And nature sure will now be kind to all.
  She has a quarrel in it, a cruel law
  Seeks to prevent her, she'll therefore fight in it
  And draw out life even to her longest thread.*   295
  Thou art scarce fifty-five.*

ANTIGONA   So many morrows!
  Those five remaining years I'll turn to days,
  To hours, or minutes, for thy company.
  'Tis fit that you and I, being man and wife,   300
  Should walk together arm in arm.

SIMONIDES   [*Aside*]
  I hope they'll go together, I would they would, i'faith,
  Then would her thirds be saved too. [*Turns to Creon*]
              The day goes away, sir.

CREON   Why, would'st thou have me gone, Simonides?

SIMONIDES
  Oh, my heart, would you have me gone before you, sir? 305

280 *filial* belonging to a son
283 *dissemble* feign, pretend   290 *behind* still to come
303 *thirds* that part of the personal property of a deceased
husband allowed to his widow. Also, the third of his real
property to which his widow might be legally entitled for
her life (OED).

You give me such a deadly wound.

CLEANTHES   [*Aside*]
  Fine rascal!

SIMONIDES   Blemish my duty so with such a question?
  Sir, I would haste me to the duke for mercy,
  He that's above the law may mitigate   310
  The rigour of the law. How a good meaning
  May be corrupted by misconstruction!

CREON
  Thou corrupt'st mine, I did not think thou meanest so.

CLEANTHES   [*Aside*]
  You were in the more error.

SIMONIDES   The words wounded me.   315

CLEANTHES   [*Aside*]
  'Twas pity thou died'st not.

SIMONIDES   I have been ransacking the helps of law,
  Conferring with these learned advocates,
  If any scruple, cause, or wrested sense
  Could have been found out to preserve your life, 320
  It had been bought though with your full estate;
  Your life's so precious to me. But, there is none.

1 LAWYER   Sir, we have canvassed it from top to toe,
  Turned it upside down, threw her on her side,
  Nay, opened and dissected all her entrails,   325
  Yet can find none. There's nothing to be hoped

308 *Blemish . . . a question?* 'You mar my reverence for you
with such a question.'
310 *mitigate* abate the severity of.
316 *on't* of it
317 *I have . . . of law* 'I have been investigating all legal
remedies'
318 *advocates* lawyers
319 *scruple* uncertainty
319 *wrested* contorted
323 *canvassed* perused
325 *entrails* clauses and phrases

But the duke's mercy.

SIMONIDES   *[Aside]*
  I know the hope of that,
  He did not make the law for that purpose.

CREON   Then to his hopeless mercy last I go.   330
  I have so many precedents before me,
  I must call it hopeless. Antigona,
  See me delivered up unto my deathsman,
  And then we'll part; five years hence* I'll look for thee.

SIMONIDES   *[Aside]*
  I hope she'll not stay so long behind you.   335

CREON   Do not bait him an hour by grief and sorrow,
  Since there's a day prefixed, haste it not.
  Suppose me sick, Antigona, dying now,
  Any disease thou wilt may be my end,
  Or when death's slow to come, say tyrants send.   340
                 Exeunt [CREON *and* ANTIGONA]

SIMONIDES   Cleanthes, if you want money, tomorrow use me;
  I'll trust you while your father's dead.
                 Exeunt [SIMONIDES *and lawyers*]

CLEANTHES   Why, here's a villain
  Able to corrupt a thousand by example!
  Does the kind root bleed out his livelihood   345
  In parent distribution to his branches,
  Adorning them with all his glorious fruits,
  Proud that his pride is seen when he's unseen?
  And must not gratitude descend again
  To comfort his old limbs in fruitless winter?   350

331 *precedents* previous examples
333 *deathsman* executioner
336 *bait* abate, hold back
337 *prefixed* already settled on
339 *wilt* wish to choose
341 *use* take advantage of
342 *while* until
345 *kind root* kindred, or perhaps benevolent father
348 *pride* the object of his pride; family
350 *fruitless winter* old age; a time no longer fruitful

Improvident, [or] at least partial Nature,
Weak woman in this kind, who in thy last
Teeming still forgets the former, ever making
The burden of thy last throes the dearest
Darling; oh yet in noble man reform it,   355
And make us better than those vegetives
Whose souls die within 'em.* Nature, as thou art old,
If love and justice be not dead in thee,
Make some the pattern of thy piety
Lest all do turn unnaturally against thee,   360
And thou be blamed for our oblivions
                    Enter LEONIDES *and* HIPPOLITA
And brutish reluctations! Aye, here's the ground
Whereon my filial faculties must build
An edifice of honour or of shame
To all mankind.   365

HIPPOLITA [*To* LEONIDES]
   You must avoid it, sir,
If there be any love within yourself.
This is far more than fate of a lost game
That another venture may restore again;
It is your life, which you should not subject   370
To any cruelty if you can preserve it.

CLEANTHES   Oh dearest woman, thou hast now doubled
   A thousand times thy nuptial dowry to me!

351 *improvident* unforeseeing
351 *partial* inclined to favour one over the other
353 *teeming* breeding
353 *still* on every occasion
354 *burden* offspring
354 *last throes* most recent labour (as in childbirth)
356 *vegetives* (reduced form of vegetative [s]) an organic
body capable of growth and development but devoid of
sensation and thought (*Obs*. OED)
359 *pattern* an example or model of particular excellence
(OED)
361 *oblivions* heedlessness
362 *reluctations* struggles; resistance (OED)
364 *edifice* monument
369 *venture* wager
372-3 *Oh dearest woman . . . dowry to me!* 'You have in love
doubled the monies which you brought with you into
marriage.'

Why, she whose love is but derived from me,
Is got before me in my debted duty.*   375

HIPPOLITA   Are you thinking such a resolution, sir?

CLEANTHES   Sweetest Hippolita, what love taught thee
To be so forward in so good a cause?

HIPPOLITA   Mine own pity, sir, did first instruct me,
And then your love and power did both command me.   380

CLEANTHES   They were all blessed angels to direct thee
And take their counsel. [*Turns to* LEONIDES] How do
                                                    you fare, sir?

LEONIDES   Never better, Cleanthes, I have conceived
Such a new joy within this old bosom
As I did never think would there have entered.   385

CLEANTHES   Joy call you it! Alas, 'tis sorrow, sir,
The worst of all sorrows, sorrow unto death.

LEONIDES
Death? What's that, Cleanthes, I thought not on it;
I was in contemplation of this woman.
'Tis all thy comfort, son; thou hast in her   390
A treasure invaluable, keep her safe.
When I die, sure 'twill be a gentle death,
For I will die with wonder of her virtues,
Nothing else shall dissolve me.

CLEANTHES   'Twere much better, sir,   395
Could you prevent their malice.

LEONIDES   I'll prevent 'em
And die the way I told thee, in the wonder
Of this good woman. I tell thee there's few men
Have such a child; I must thank thee for her.   400
That the strong tie of wedlock should do more

396 *prevent* evade
397 *prevent* (Theol.) go before with spiritual guidance and
help: said of God, or of his grace anticipating human action
and need (*arch*. OED)
401 *strong* ed. (stronger Q)

Than nature in her nearest ligaments
Of blood and propagation! I should ne'er
Have begot such a daughter of my own.
A daughter-in-law? Law were above nature   405
Were there more such children.*

CLEANTHES   This admiration
Helps nothing to your safety; think of that, sir.

LEONIDES   Had you heard her, Cleanthes, but labour
In the search of means to save my forfeit life,   410
And knew the wise and sound preservations
That she found out, you would redouble all
My wonder in your love to her.

CLEANTHES   The thought,
The very thought claims all that from me   415
And she's now possessed of it. But, good sir,
If you have aught received from her advice,
Let's follow it, or else let's better think
And take the surest course.

LEONIDES   I'll tell thee one: 420
She counsels me to fly my severe country,
Turn all into treasure, and there build up
My decaying fortunes in a safer soil,
Where Epire's law cannot claim me.

CLEANTHES   And, sir,   425
I apprehend it as a safest course,
And may be easily accomplished.
Let us be all most expeditious;
Every country where we breathe will be our own
Or better soil. Heaven is the roof of all,   430
And now, as Epire's situate by this law,
There is 'twixt us and heaven a dark eclipse.

HIPPOLITA   Oh then avoid it, sir; these sad events
Follow those black predictions.

LEONIDES   I prithee, peace!   435

411 *preservations* advice for keeping from injury (OED)
426 *apprehend* perceive, recognize
428 *expeditious* speedy
431 *situate* subject to the circumstances of
432 *eclipse* obscuration of light

I do allow thy love, Hippolita,
But must not follow it as counsel, child;
I must not shame my country for the law.
This country here hath bred me, brought me up,
And shall I now refuse a grave in her?   440
I'm in my second infancy, and children
Ne'er sleep so sweetly in their nurse's cradle
As in their natural mother's.

HIPPOLITA   Ay, but sir,
She is unnatural; then the stepmother   445
Is to be preferred before her.

LEONIDES   Tush! She shall
Allow it me despite of her entrails.
Why, do you think how far from judgement 'tis
That I should travel forth to seek a grave   450
That is already digged for me at home,
Nay, perhaps find it in my way to seek it.
Now have I then sought a repentant sorrow?
For your dear loves, how have I banished you
From your country ever? With my base attempt,   455
How have I beggared you in wasting that
Which only for your sakes I bred together?
Buried my name in Epire, which I built
Upon this frame to live forever in?
What a base coward shall I be to fly   460
From that enemy which every minute meets me,
And thousand odds he had not long vanquished me
Before this hour of battle! Fly my death?
I will not be so false unto your states,
Nor fainting to the man that's yet in me;   465
I'll meet him bravely. I cannot, this knowing, fear
That when I am gone hence, I shall be here.

436 *allow* approve
447-8 *She shall . . . her entrails.* 'She shall give me any
due in spite of her present constitution.'
453 *repentant sorrow* contrite distress
456 *beggared* impoverished
459 *frame* order
459 *to live forever in* to achieve remembrance by
461 *that enemy* death
462 *And thousand odds* it has been against a thousand odds
467 *I shall be there* i.e. dead, rather than living in
some alien land.

Come, I have days of preparation left.

CLEANTHES   Good sir, hear me;
  I have a genius that has prompted me   470
  And I have almost formed it into words.
  'Tis done, pray you observe 'em; I can conceal you
  And you not leave your country.

LEONIDES   Tush, it cannot be
  Without a certain peril on us all.   475

CLEANTHES   Danger must be hazarded rather than accept
  A sure destruction. You have a lodge, sir,
  So far remote from way of passengers
  That seldom any mortal eye does greet with it;
  And, yes, so sweetly situate with thickets,   480
  Built with such cunning labrynths within,
  As if the provident heavens, foreseeing cruelty,
  Had bid you frame it to this purpose only.

LEONIDES   Fie, fie, 'tis dangerous, and treason too,
  To abuse the law.   485

HIPPOLITA   'Tis holy care, sir,
  Of your dear life, which is your own to keep
  But not your own to lose, either in will
  Or negligence.

CLEANTHES   Call you it treason, sir?   490
  I had been then a traitor unto you
  Had I forgot this. Beseech you, accept of it;
  It is secure and a duty to yourself.

LEONIDES   What a coward will you make me!

CLEANTHES   You mistake,   495

This is another troublesome line. This textual emendation
is designed to make clear Leonides' preference to die
honourably in Epire rather than live dishonourably on alien
soil.
470 *genius* attendant spirit
473 *you* ed. (yet Q)
476 *hazarded* risked
481 *labrynths* winding paths obscured by high hedges; mazes
482 *provident* prudent

'Tis noble courage! Now you fight with death
And yield not to him till you stoop under him.

LEONDIES   This must needs open to discovery,
And then what torture follows?

CLEANTHES   By what means, sir?   500
Why, there's but one body in all this counsel
Which cannot betray itself. We two are one,
One soul, one body, one heart, that think all one thought;
And yet we two are not completely one,
But as [I] have derived myself from you.   505
Who shall betray us where there is no second?*

HIPPOLITA   You must not mistrust my faith, though my sex
Plead weak[ness] and frailty for me.

LEONIDES   Oh, I dare not!
But where's the means that must make answer for me?   510
I cannot be lost without a full account,
And what must pay that reckoning?

CLEANTHES   Oh, sir, we will
Keep solemn obits for your funeral;
We'll seem to weep and seem to joy withall   515
That death so gently has prevented you
The law's sharp rigour; and this no mortal ear
Shall participate the knowledge of.

LEONIDES   Ha, ha, ha,
This will be a sportive fine demur   520
If the error be not found.

CLEANTHES   Pray doubt of none.
Your company and best provision
Must be no further furnished than by us,

510 *means* intermediary agent
511 *account* explanation
512 *reckoning* enumeration
514 *obits* obsequies
516 *prevented* debarred
518 *participate* share
520 *sportive* diverting, frolicsome
520 *demur* delay

And, in the interim, your solitude   525
May converse with heaven, and fairly prepare
[For that] which was too violent and raging
Thrown headlong on you.

LEONIDES   Still there are some doubts
Of the discovery, yet I do allow it.   530

HIPPOLITA   Will you not mention now the cost and charge
Which will be in your keeping.

LEONIDES   That will be somewhat
Which you might save, too.

CLEANTHES   With his will against him,   535
What foe is more to man than man himself?
Are you resolved, sir?

LEONIDES   I am, Cleanthes,
If by this means I do get a reprieve
And cozen death a while, when he shall come   540
Armed in his own power to give the blow,
I'll smile upon him then, and laughing go.
Exeunt [omnes]

529 *Still* Although
534 *save* avoid
540 *cozen* cheat

Act II scene i

Enter Duke [EVANDER], *three courtiers, and* [*the*]
executioner, [CRATILUS.].

EVANDER   Executioner!

CRATILUS   My lord.

EVANDER   How did old Diocles take his death?

CRATILUS
    As weeping brides receive their joys at night, my lord,
    With trembling yet with patience.   5

EVANDER   Why, 'twas well.

1 COURTIER
    Nay, I knew my father would do well, my lord,
    Whene'er he came to die. I'd that opinion of him.
    Which made me the more willing to part from him.
    He was not fit to live in the world, indeed,   10
    Any time these ten years, my lord,
    But I would not say so much.

EVANDER   No! You did not well in it,
    For he that's all spent is ripe for death at all hours,
    And does but trifle time out.   15

1 COURTIER   Troth, my lord,
    I would I had known your mind nine years ago.

EVANDER   Our law is fourscore years because we judge
    Dotage complete then, as unfruitfulness
    In women at threescore. Marry, if the son   20
    Can within compass bring good solid proofs
    Of his own father's weakness and unfitness
    To live or sway the living, though he want five
    Or ten years of his number, that's not it;

11 *these ten years* these past ten years
15 *trifle* waste
16 *Troth* in truth
19 *dotage* senility
21 *within compass* within due limits

His defect makes him fourscore and 'tis fit
He dies when he deserves, for every act
Is in effect then, when the cause is ripe.

2 COURTIER   [*Drawing the other courtiers aside*]
An admirable prince! How rarely he talks!
Oh that we'd known this, lads! What a time did we endure
In two-penny commons,* and in boots twice vamped!   30

1 COURTIER
Now we have two pair a week, and yet not thankful;
'Twill be a fine world for them, sirs, that come after us.

2 COURTIER   Aye, and they knew it.

1 COURTIER   Peace! Let them never know it.

3 COURTIER
A pox, there be young heirs will soon smell it out.   35

2 COURTIER   'Twill come to 'em by instinct, man. [*Turns
back to* EVANDER] May your grace
Never be old, you stand so well for youth.

EVANDER   Why, now, methinks our court looks like a spring;
Sweet, fresh, and fashionable, now the old weeds are gone.

1 COURTIER   'Tis as a court should be: 40
Gloss and good clothes, my lord, no matter for merit;
And herein your law proves a provident act,
When men pass not the palsy of their tongues,
Nor colour in their cheeks.

25 *defect* imperfection
30 *vamped* patched
33 *and* if
33-4 *Aye, and they . . . . know it.* Q gives both these
lines to the second Courtier
38 *a spring* a young, fresh outpouring
41 *Gloss* superficial lustre
41 *matter* care
42 *provident* prudent
42 *a provident act* ed. (a provident act, my lord Q)
43 *pass* convey
43 *palsy* impairment, paralysis

EVANDER   But women by that law should live long,
    For they are ne'er past it.

1 COURTIER
    It will have heats though, when they see the painting
    Go an inch deep in the wrinkle, and take up
    A box more than their gossips. But for men, my lord,
    That should be the sole bravery of a palace,   50
    To walk with hollow eyes and long white beards,
    As if a prince dwelt in a land of goats;
    With clothes as if they sat upon their backs on purpose
    To arraign a fashion, and condemn it to exile;
    Their pockets in their sleeves, as if they laid
    Their ear to avarice and heard the devil whisper.
    Now ours lie downward, here, close to the flank,
    Right spending pockets as a son's should be
    That lives in the fashion. Where our diseased fathers,
    Wood with the sciatica and aches,   60
    Brought up your pan's hose first, which ladies laughed at,
    Giving no reverence to the place, lie ruined.
    They love a doublet that's three hours a-buttoning,
    And fits so close makes a man groan again
    And his soul mutter half a day. Yet these are those   65
    That carry sway and worth. Pricked up in clothes,
    Why should we fear our rising?

47 *have heats*   ed. be lively (heates Q)
49 *box*   cosmetic case
49 *gossips*   lady friends
50 *bravery*   splendour
54 *arraign*   indict
59 *where*   whereas
60 *wood*   mad
60 *wood*   ed. (would Q)
60 *sciatica*   a disease characterized by pain in the great
sciatic nerve and its branches (OED)
61 *pan'd*   fashioned from material made of narrow strips of
varied coloured cloth joined together.
62 *lie*   ed. (lies Q)
65 *soul*   spirit, movement
66 *prick'd up* **attired** elaborately
67 *fear our rising*   have apprehensions about advance in
influence and station

EVANDER   You but wrong
  Our **kindness** and your own desserts to doubt on it.
  Has not our law made you rich before your time?   70
  Our countenance then can make you honourable.

1 COURTIER   We'll spare for no cost, sir, to appear worthy.

EVANDER   Why, you're in the noble way then, for the most
  Are but appearers; worth itself, it is lost
  And bravery stands for it.   75
                    Enter CREON, ANTIGONA *and* SIMONIDES

1 COURTIER   Look, look, who comes here!
  I smell death and another courtier.
  Simonides!

2 COURTIER   Sim!

SIMONIDES   Push! I'm not for you yet;   80
  Your company's too costly; after the old man's
  Dispatched, I shall have time to talk with you.
  I shall come into the fashion [too], ye shall see
  After a day or two. In the meantime,
  I am not for your company.   85

EVANDER   Old Creon, you have been expected long,
  Sure you're above fourscore.

SIMONIDES   Upon my life
  Not four-and-twenty hours, my lord, I searched
  The church-book yesterday. Does your grace think   90
  I'd let my father wrong the law, my lord?
  'Twere pity o' my life then! No, your act
  Shall not receive a minute's wrong by him
  While I live, sir; and he's so just himself too,
  I know he would no[t] offer it. Here he stands.   95

CREON   'Tis just
  I die, indeed, my lord; for I confess

71 *countenance* favour, sanction
75 *bravery* display, show
80 *Push!* an exclamation of disdain (*Obs.* pish)
83 *ye shall see* ed. (yee shall see too Q)
90 *church-book* register of births
92 *o'* ed. (a' Q)

I'm troublesome to life now, and the state
Can hope for nothing worthy from me now,
Either in force or counsel. I've of late   100
Employed myself quite from the world, and he
That once begins to serve his Maker faithfully,
Can never serve a worldly prince well after;*
'Tis clean another way.

ANTIGONA   Oh, give not confidence
    To all he speaks, my lord, in his own injury!   105
    His preparation only for the next world
    Makes him talk wildly to his wrong of this.
    He is not lost in judgement –

SIMONIDES [*Aside*]
    She spoils all again.   110

ANTIGONA   Deserving any way for state employment.

SIMONIDES   Mother!

ANTIGONA
    His very household laws prescribed at home by him
    Are able to conform seven Christian kingdoms,*
    They are so wise and virtuous.   115

SIMONIDES [*Tries to interrupt*]
    Mother, I say –

ANTIGONA   I know your laws extend not to desert, sir,
    But to unnecessary years, and, my lord,
    His are not such. Though they show white, they're worthy,
    Judicious, able, and religious.   120

SIMONIDES [*To* ANTIGONA]
    I'll help you to a courtier of nineteen, mother.

100 *in force or counsel*   as a soldier or as advisor
100 *of late*   ed. (alate Q)
105 *confidence*   trust
113 *prescribed*   ordained
114 *to conform*   to bring into harmony
117 *desert*   merit; excellence

ANTIGONA   [*To* SIMONIDES]
Away, unnatural!

SIMONIDES   [*To* ANTIGONA]
Then I am no fool I'm sure,
For to be natural at such a time
Were a fool's part indeed.   125

ANTIGONA   Your grace's pity, sir!
And 'tis but fit and just.

CREON   The law, my lord,
And that's the justest way.

SIMONIDES   [*Aside*]
Well said, father, i'faith,   130
Thou wert ever juster than my mother still.

EVANDER   Come hither, sir.

SIMONIDES   My lord.

EVANDER   What are those orders?

ANTIGONA   Worth observation, sir,   135
So please you hear them read.

SIMONIDES   [*Whispers to* EVANDER]
The woman speaks she knows not what, my lord.
He make a law, poor man! He bought a table, indeed,
Only to learn to die by it. There's the business now
Wherein there are some precepts for a son too,   140
How he should learn to live, but I ne'er looked upon it;
For when he's dead I shall live well enough
And keep a better table than that, I trow.

EVANDER   And is that all, sir?

SIMONIDES   All, I vow, my lord,   145

138 *table* tablet; a large sheet of paper on which rules for
daily living were inscribed; also alluding to the tables of
stone upon which Moses received the Commandments.
140 *precepts* commandments
143 *table* provisions of meat and drink; the guests at the
dining table (Pun on *table* 1. 138).

Save a few running admonitions
Upon cheese-trenchers,* as -
  Take heed of whoring, shun it,
  Tis like a cheese too strong of the runnet,* -
And such calves' maws of wit and admonition   150
Good to catch mice with, but not sons and heirs;
They're not so easily caught.

EVANDER   [*turns to executioner*]
  Agent for death.

CRATILUS   Your will, my lord?

EVANDER   Take hence that pile of years   155
  Before [he] surfeit with unprofitable age,
  And with the rest, from the high promontory,
  Cast him into the sea.

CREON   'Tis noble justice!
                              [*Exeunt* CRATILUS *with* CREON]

ANTIGONA   'Tis cursed tyranny!   160

SIMONIDES   Peace! Take heed, mother,
  You have but a short time to be cast down yourself,*
  And let a young courtier do it, and you be wise
  In the meantime.

ANTIGONA   Hence, slave!   165

SIMONIDES   Well, seven-and-fifty,   [*Exit* ANTIGONA]
  You've but three years to scold,* then comes your payment.

1 COURTIER   Simonides.

SIMONIDES
  Push, I'm not brave enough to hold you talk yet;

146 *admonitions* warnings
147 *trenchers* wooden or metal plates (see notes ll. 146-7)
149 *runnet* rennet; a mass of curdled milk found in the
stomach of an unweaned calf or any other animal, used for
curdling milk in making cheese (OED)
150 *calves' maws* calves' stomachs

Give a man time, I have a suit a-making.   170
                              Recorders [sound from above]

2 COURTIER
  We love thy form first, brave clothes will come, man.

SIMONIDES
  I'll make 'em come else, with a mischief to 'em
  As other gallants do that have less left 'em.
                              Recorders [sound again]

EVANDER   Hark, whence those sounds? What's that?
Enter CLEANTHES *and* HIPPOLITA, [*smiling and brightly
dressed,*] *with a hearse.*

1 COURTIER Some funeral   175
  It seems, my lord, and young Cleanthes follows.

EVANDER   Cleanthes!

2 COURTIER   'Tis, my lord, and in the place
  Of a chief mourner, too, but strangely habited.

EVANDER   Yet suitable to his behaviour, mark it;   180
  He comes all the way smiling, do ycu observe it?
  I never saw a corpse so joyfully followed.
  Light colours and light cheeks! Who should this be?
  'Tis a thing worth resolving.

SIMONIDES   One belike that doth participate   185
  In this our present joy.

EVANDER   Cleanthes!

CLEANTHES [*Laughing and smiling*]
  Oh, my lord!

EVANDER [*To the courtiers*]
  He laughed outright now!

170 *a suit a-making* a plan in the works
171 *form* method; fashion
171 *brave* fashionable; splendid
172 *else* or else
172 *mischief* deviltry
179 *habited* dressed

Was ever such a contrariety seen   190
In natural courses yet, nay, professed openly?

1 COURTIER
  I ha[ve] known a widow laugh closely, my lord,
  Under her handkercher, when t'other part
  Of her old face has wept like rain in sunshine;*
  But all the face to laugh apparently,   195
  Was never seen yet.

SIMONIDES   Yes, mine did once.

CLEANTHES   'Tis of a heavy time, the joyfullest day
  That ever son was born to.

EVANDER   How can that be?   200

CLEANTHES   I joy to make it plain, my father's dead.

EVANDER   Dead!

2 COURTIER   Old Leonides?

CLEANTHES   In his last month dead;
  He beguiled cruel law the sweetliest   205
  That ever age was blest to.
  It grieves me that a tear should fall upon it,
  Being a thing so joyful, but his memory
  Will work it out, I see. When his poor heart broke,
  I did not so much but leaped for joy
  So mountingly, I touched the stars, methought.
  I would not hear of blacks, I was so light,
  But chose a colour orient, like my mind;
  For blacks are often such dissembling mourners
  There is no credit given to it. It has lost   215
  All reputation by false sons and widows.
  Now I would have men know what I resemble,

190 *contrariety* opposition of one thing to another in
nature, quality, or action (OED)
191 *natural courses* the ordinary pattern of events or
behaviour   205 *beguiled* deceived; cheated
205 *sweetliest* in the most pleasing manner
213 *orient* as in orient pearl: brilliant; lustrous
214 *dissembling* feigning; simulating

A truth, indeed; 'tis joy clad like a joy,
Which is more honest than a cunning grief
That's only faced with sables for a show,   220
But gaudy-hearted. When I saw death come
So ready to deceive you, sir, forgive me,
I could not choose but be entirely merry.*
And yet, to see now, of a sudden
Naming but death, I show myself a mortal   225
That's never constant to one passion long;
I wonder whence that tear came when I smiled
In the production on it. Sorrow's a thief
That can, when joy looks on, steal forth a grief.*
But gracious leave, my lord, when I have performed,   230
My last poor duty to my father's bones.
I shall return your servant.

EVANDER   Well, perform it.
   The law is satisfied, they can but die.   235
   And, by his death, Cleanthes, you gain well
   A rich and fair revenue. *Flourish*
   [*Exeunt* DUKE EVANDER *and courtiers*]

SIMONIDES   I would I had even another father
   Condition he did the like.

CLEANTHES   [*Aside*]
   I have passed it bravely! How blest was I   240
   To have the Duke in sight! Now 'tis confirmed;
   Past fear of doubts confirmed. [*To the funeral
   procession, loudly*] On, on, I say,
   He that brought me to man, I bring to clay.*
                [*Exeunt funeral procession,
            followed by* CLEANTHES *and* HIPPOLITA]

219 *cunning* deceitful
220 *sables* mourning garments; a suit of black worn as an
emblem of grief (OED)
221 *gaudy-hearted* filled with joy
238 *condition* on condition that
239 *bravely* splendidly; in a worthy manner
239 *How* ed. (Now how Q)
240 *To have the Duke in sight* ed. (To have the dim sight
Q. Gifford suggests the manuscript probably read "To
have the d in sight")
240 *confirmed* firmly established

SIMONIDES   I'm wrapped now in a contemplation
    Even at the very sight of yonder hearse!
    I do but think what a fine thing 'tis now   245
    To live and follow some seven uncles thus,
    As many cousin-germans, and such people
    That will leave legacies. A pox! I'd see 'em hanged else
    E'er I'd follow one of them and they could find the way.
    Now I've enough to begin to be horrible convetous.   250
    Enter [CREON'S servants]: Butler, Tailor, Bailiff,
    Cook, Coachman, and Footman

BUTLER   We come to know your worship's pleasure, sir;
    Having long served your father, how your good will
    Stands towards our entertainment.

SIMONIDES   Not a jot, i'faith:
    My father wore cheap garments, he might do it;   255
    I shall have all my clothes come home tomorrow.
    They will eat up all you, and there were
                                more of you, sirs,
    To keep you six at livery, and still munching!*

TAILOR   Why, I'm a tailor, you've most need of me, sir.

SIMONIDES   Thou madest my father's clothes, that I   260
    confess, but what son and heir will have his father's
    tailor unless he have a mind to be well laughed at.
    Thou hast been so used to wide long side things, that
    when I come to truss, I shall have the waist of my
    doublet lie upon my buttocks. A sweet sight!   265

243 *contemplation* musing; wonderment
247 *cousin-germans* first cousins
253 *entertainment* service; employment (*Obs.* OED)
257 *eat up* use up the time of   257 *and* if
258 *livery* Pun; the distinctive uniform worn by a particular man's servants; the keeping 'at livery,' the feeding
and grooming of a horse.
264 *to truss* to tie the 'points' or laces with which the
hose were fastened to the doublet (*Obs.* OED)
264 *doublet* a closely-fitting body-garment, with or without
sleeves, worn by men from the 14th to 18th centuries
(*Obs.* OED)

BUTLER   I, a butler

SIMONIDES
    There's least need of thee, fellow, I shall ne'er drink
    at home, I shall be so drunk abroad.

BUTLER
    But a cup of small beer will do well next morning, sir.

SIMONIDES
    I grant you, but what need I keep so big a knave for   270
    a cup of small beer?

COOK
    Butler, you have your answer. Marry, sir, a cook I know
    your mastership cannot be without.

SIMONIDES
    The more ass art thou to think so, for what should I do
    with a mountebank, no drink in my house? The banishing
    the butler might have been a warning for thee, unless
    thou meanest to choke me.   277

COOK   In the meantime you have choked me, methinks.

BAILIFF
    These are superfluous vanities, indeed, and so accounted
    of in these days, sir; but then, your bailiff to receive
    your rents?   281

SIMONIDES
    I prithee, hold thy tongue, fellow, I shall take a course
    to spend'em faster than thou canst reckon'em. 'Tis not
    the rents must serve my turn, unless I mean to be laughed
    at; if a man should be seen out of slash-me,* let him   285
    ne'er look to be a right gallant. [*Turns to coachman
    and footman*] But, sirrah, with whom is your business?

269 *small beer* weak or inferior beer
275 *mountebank* a pretender to skills he does not possess
277 *choke* to have the air cut off from having dry food
caught in the throat
278 *choked* cut off communication
280 *bailiff* an agent who collects his lord's rents
285 *out of slash-me* out of style (see notes)

COACHMAN   Your good mastership.

SIMONIDES
You have stood silent all this while, like men that know
their strengths. In these days none of you can want 290
employment; you can win me wagers, footman, in
running races.

FOOTMAN   I dare boast it, sir.

SIMONIDES   And when my bets are all come in and store,
Then, coachman, you can hurry me to my whore.   295

COACHMAN   I'll firk'em into foam else.

SIMONIDES [He] speaks brave matter!
And I'll firk some too, or shall cost hot water.*
[*Exeunt* SIMONIDES, *footman, and coachman*]

COOK
Why, here's an age to make a cook a ruffian and scald
the devil! Indeed, do strange mad things, make   300
muttom-pasties of dog's flesh, bake snakes for lamprey
pies, and cats for conies!

BUTLER
Come, will you be ruled by a butler's advice once?
For we must make up our fortunes somewhere now, as the
case stands. Let's even, therefore, go seek out windows
    305

291-2 *but you can win me . . . running races.* As evidence
for his dating of *The Old Law* 1618, Baldwin Maxwell cites
a letter from John Chamberlain to Sir Dudley Carleton
(April 10, 1618) in which Chamberlain describes a race
between two footmen from St. Albans to Clerkenwell. Much
money was won and lost in betting; in fact, "my lord of
Buckingham, for his part, went away with £3000." The race
attracted such attention that "all the court" and "the
king himself" went to see the finish. "As many people"
turned out "as at the king's first coming to London."
One such notorious race, Baldwin concludes, would certainly give rise to Simonides humerous reference (*Studies in
Beaumont, Fletcher, and Massinger*, 1939, 144-5).
296 *I'll firk'em into a foam else.* 'Otherwise I'll whip
the horses into a lather.'
299 *ruffian* a man of low degree
301 *lamprey* eel   302 *conies* rabbits

of nine and fifty and we can; that's within a year of
their deaths and so we shall be sure to be quickly rid
of 'em, for a year's enough of conscience to be troubled
with a wife for any man living.

COOK

  Oracle butler! oracle butler! He puts down all   310
  the doctors o' the name!* *Exeunt omnes*

306 *and we can*   if we can

                    Act II, scene ii

Enter EUGENIA *and* PARTHENIA

EUGENIA   Parthenia.

PARTHENIA   Mother.

EUGENIA [*Aside*]
    I shall be troubled
    This six months with an old clog! Would the law
    Had been cut one year shorter!   5

PARTHENIA   Did you call, forsooth?

EUGENIA
    Yes, you must make some spoonmeat for your father,
    And warm three nightcaps for him. [*Exit* PARTHENIA]
                                    Out upon it!
    The mere conceit turns a young woman's stomach.
    His slippers must be warmed in August too,   10
    And his gown girt to him in the very dogdays*
    When every mastiff lolls out his tongue for heat.
    Would not this vex a beauty of nineteen now?
    Alas! I should be tumbling in cold baths,
    Under each armpit a fine bean-flour bag   15
    To screw out whiteness when I list;
    And some seven of the properest men in the dukedom
    Making a banquet ready in the next room for me,
    Where he that gets the first kiss is envied
    And stands upon his guard a fortnight after.   20

4 *clog* encumbrance
7 *spoonmeat* soft or liquid food
8 *nightcaps* drinks taken to induce sleep
9 *conceit* notion   11. *girt* securely fastened
14 *I should be tumbling in cold baths* ed. (I shall be
tumbling in cold Bathes now Q)
15 *bean-flour bag* ed. (bean-flower bag Q) a cloth sack with
a flour made from ground beans which, when patted on the
skin, gave off a fine talcum-like powder.
16 *when I list* 'when I please;' or perhaps there is a pun
intended here from 'when I lust (desire).'
17 *properest* most suitable; most fitting
20 *stands upon his guard* Pun; is wary of his life: main-
tains an erection (see below 1.22)

This is life for nineteen! 'Tis but justice,
For old men, whose great acts stand in their minds
And nothing in their bodies, do ne'er think
A woman young enough for their desire;
And we young wenches that have mother wits   25
And love to marry muck first, and man after,
Do never think old men are old enough
That we may soon be rid of 'em. There's our quittance!
I have waited for the happy hour this two year,
And if death be so unkind still to let him live,   30
All that time I am lost. *Enter courtiers [elaborately
groomed]*

1 COURTIER   Young lady!

2 COURTIER   Oh sweet precious bud of beauty!
Troth, she smells over all the house, methinks.

1 COURTIER   The sweetbriar's but a counterfeit to her! 35
It does exceed you only in the prickle,
But that it shall not long, if you'll be ruled, lady.*

EUGENIA   What means this sudden visitation, gentlemen?
So passing well performed* too! Who's your milliner?

1 COURTIER   Love and thy beauty, widow.   40

EUGENIA   Widow, sir?

1 COURTIER
'Tis sure, and that's as good. In truth, we're suitors,
We come a-wooing, wench, plain dealing's best.

EUGENIA   A-wooing? What, before my husband's dead!

21 *but* ed. (but 'tis Q)
22 *stand* remain steadfast; the punning inherent in 1. 20
is continued here. Eugenia also means that any sexual
potential old men may have is all in their minds.
25 *mother wits* basic inclinations; the word *mother*, when
it is linked with *muck*(1. 26) may also mean scummy
39 *milliner* A vendor of 'fancy' wares and articles of
apparel, especially of such as were originally of Milan
manufacture, e.g. 'Milan bonnets, 'ribbons, gloves, cutlery
(*Obs*. OED).

2 COURTIER
   Let's lose no time. Six months will have an end, you know,
   I know it by all the bonds that e'er I made yet.   46

EUGENIA
   That's a sure knowledge, but it holds not here, sir.

1 COURTIER   Do not we know the craft of you young tumblers?
   That [when] you wed an old man, you think upon
   Another husband as you are marrying of him?   50
   We, knowing your thought, made bold to see you.

EUGENIA   [*Aside*]
   How wondrous right he speaks! 'Twas my thought indeed.
   Enter SIMONIDES [*elegantly dressed, and*] *coachman*

SIMONIDES   By your leave, sweet widow, do you lack
   any gallants?

EUGENIA [*Aside*]
   Widow again! 'Tis a comfort to be called so.

1 COURTIER   Who's this? Simonides?   55

2 COURTIER   Brave Sim, i'faith!

SIMONIDES   Coachman.

COACHMAN   Sir?

SIMONIDES   Have an especial care of my new mares.
   They say, sweet widow, he that loves a horse well   60
   Must needs love a widow well.* When dies thy husband?
   Is it not July next?

EUGENIA   Oh, you're too hot, sir,
   Pray cool yourself and take September with you!

46 *bonds* assignations to repay monies owed
48 *we* ed. (you Q)
48 *craft* cunning
48 *you* ed. (your Q)
48 *tumblers* women who are easily tossed about in bed
53 *gallants* men to pay court; paramours

SIMONIDES   September! Oh, I was but two bows wide.   65

1 COURTIER   Master Simonides!

SIMONIDES   I can entreat you, gallants, I'm in fashion too.
    Enter LISANDER

LISANDER   Ha! Whence this herd of folly? What are you?

SIMONIDES
    Well-willers to your wife; pray tend your book, sir.
    We have nothing to say to you; you may go die   70
    For here be those in place that can supply.

LISANDER   What's thy wild business here?

SIMONIDES   Old man, I'll tell thee,
    I come to beg the reversion of thy wife;
    I think these gallants be of my mind too.   75
    Thou art but a dead man; therefore,
    What should a man do talking with thee.
    Come, widow, stand to your tackling.

LISANDER   Impious bloodhounds!

SIMONIDES   Let the ghost talk, ne'er mind him.   80

LISANDER   Shames of nature!

SIMONIDES   Alas, poor ghost!* Consider what the man is.

LISANDER   [*With extreme anger*]
    Monsters unnatural! You that have been covetous
    Of your own fathers' deaths, gape ye for mine now?
    Cannot a poor old man that now can reckon

65 *but two bows wide* to draw the long bow - to make
exaggerated statements (OED); thus, 'I was just making an
extravagant guess.'
67 *entreat* pass the time with (*Obs.* OED)
69 *book* Bible; prayer book
71 *supply* fulfill your function
74 *reversion* the right of succeeding or occupying (OED)
76 *Thou* ed. (But thou Q)
78 *stand to your tackling* 'be prepared for boarding
(naut.).'

Even all the hours he has to live, live quiet
For such wild beasts as these, that neither hold
A certainty of good within themselves,
But scatter others' comforts that are ripened
For holy uses? Is hot youth so hasty   90
It will not give an old man leave to die
And leave a widow first, but will make one
The husband looking on? May your destructions
Come all in hasty figures to your souls,
Your wealth depart in haste to overtake   95
Your honesties, that died when you were infants!
May your male seed be hasty spendthrifts too,
Your daughters hasty sinners and diseased
Ere they be thought at years to welcome misery!
And may you never know what leisure is   100
But at repentance! [*Stops suddenly*]
                    I am too uncharitable,
Too foul! I must go cleanse myself with prayers.
These are the plagues of fondness to old men,
We're punished home with what we dote upon.
Exit [LISANDER]

SIMONIDES   So, so!   105
The ghost is vanished; now, your answer, lady.

EUGENIA   Excuse me, gentlemen, 'twere as much impudence
In me to give you a kind answer yet,
As madness to produce a churlish one.
I could say now, come a month hence, sweet gentlemen,110
Or two, or three, or when you will, indeed,
But I say no such thing. I set no time,
Nor is it mannerly to deny any.
I'll carry an even hand to all the world.
Let other women make what haste they will;   115
What's that to me? But I profess unfeignedly,
I'll have my husband dead before I marry.

91 *leave* liberty
94 *hasty figures* hurried numbers
96 *honesties* virtues
97 *hasty* thoughtless
98 *hasty* early ripening
103 *fondness* foolishness
109 *churlish* ungracious
114 *carry on even hand* appear straight-forward
116 *unfeignedly* without guile

Ne'er look for other answer at my hands, gentlemen.

SIMONIDES
Would he were hanged, for my part looks for other!*

EUGENIA   I'm at a word.   120

SIMONIDES   And I'm at a blow then,
I'll lay you on the lips and leave you. [*Kisses her*]

1 COURTIER   Well struck, Sim!

SIMONIDES
He that dares say he'll mend it, I'll strike him.

1 COURTIER   He would betray himself to be a botcher   125
That goes about to mend it.

EUGENIA   Gentlemen,
You know my mind. I bar you not my house;
But if you choose out hours more seasonably,
You may have entertainment. [*Re-]enter* PARENTHIA   130

SIMONIDES   [*To courtiers*]
What will she do hereafter,
When sh[e] is a widow keeps open house already?
Exeunt SIMONIDES *and courtiers*

EUGENIA   How now, girl?

PARTHENIA
Those feathered fools that hither took their flight
Have grieved my father much.   135

EUGENIA   Speak well of youth, wench,
While thou hast a day to live. 'Tis youth must make
                                                     thee,
And when youth fails, wise women will make it.
But always take age first to make thee rich;
That was my counsel ever, and then youth   140
Will make thee sport enough all thy life after.
'Tis [the] time's policy, wench. What is it to bide

124 *mend* do better than
125 *He would . . . botcher* 'Any man would be a fool'
125 *botcher* ed. (brother Q)

A little hardness for a pair of years or so?
A man whose only strength lies in his breath,
Weakness in all parts else, thy bedfellow   145
A cough of the lungs, or say a wheezing matter;
Then [to] shake off chains and dance all thy life after?

PARTHENIA   Everyone to their liking, but I say
An honest man's worth all, be he young or gray.
Enter HIPPOLITA
Yonder's my cousin. [*Exit* PARTHENIA]   150

EUGENIA   [*Aside*]
Art, I must use thee now.
Dissembling is the best help for a virtue
That ever woman had; it saves their credit often.
[*Begins to weep*]

HIPPOLITA   How now, cousin!
What, weeping?   155

EUGENIA   Can you blame me when the time
Of my dear love and husband now draws on?
I study funeral tears against the day
I must be a sad widow.

HIPPOLITA
In troth, Eugenia, I have cause to weep too;   160
But when I visit, I come comfortably
And look to be so quited. Yet more sobbing?

EUGENIA
Oh, the greatest part of your affliction's past;
The worst of mine's to come! I have one to die.
Your husband's father is dead and fixed   165
In his eternal peace, past the sharp tyrannous blow.

PARTHENIA   You must use patience, coz.

EUGENIA   Tell me of patience.

HIPPOLITA   You have example for it in me and many.

EUGENIA
Yours was a father-in-law, but mine a husband!   170

146 *wheezing* ed. (wheering Q)

Oh, for a woman that could love and live
With an old man; mine is a jewel, cousin,
So quietly he lies by one, so still.

HIPPOLITA   [*Aside*]
  Alas! I have a secret lodged within me
  Which now will out. In pity, I cannot hold.   175

EUGENIA
  One that will not disturb me in my sleep
  For a whole month together, less it be
  With those diseases age is subject to,
  As aches, coughs, and pains, and these, heaven knows,
  Against his will too. He's the quietest man,   180
  Especially in bed.

HIPPOLITA   Be comforted.

EUGENIA   How can I, lady?
  None knows the terror of a husband's loss,
  But they that fear to lose him.   185

HIPPOLITA   [*Aside*]
  Fain would I keep it in, but 'twill not be;
  She is my kinswoman and I'm pitiful.
  I must impart a good, if I know it once,
  To them that stand in need on it. I'm like one
  Loves not to banquet with a joy alone,   190
  My friends must partake too. [*Turns to* EUGENIA]
                          Prithee, cease, cousin.
  If your love be so boundless, which is rare
  In a young woman in these days, I tell you,
  To one so much past service as your husband,
  There is a way to beguile law and help you.   195
  My husband found it out first.

EUGENIA   Oh, sweet cousin!

HIPPOLITA
  You may conceal him and give out his death
  Within the time, order his funeral too;   200
  We had it so for ours, I praise heaven for it,
  And he's alive and safe!

175 *cannot* ed. (can't Q)
177 *For* ed. (After Q)
195 *beguile* cheat

EUGENIA   Oh, blessed coz,
  How thou revivest me!

HIPPOLITA   We daily see   205
  The good old man and feed him twice a day.
  Methinks it is the sweetest joy to cherish him,
  That ever life yet showed me.

EUGENIA   So should I think
  A dainty thing to nurse an old man well.   210

HIPPOLITA
  And then we have his prayers and daily blessing,
  And we two live so lovingly upon it,
  His son and I, and so contently,
  You cannot think unless you tasted on it.

EUGENIA
  No, I warrant you! Oh, loving cousin,   215
  What a great sorrow hast thou eased me of!
  A thousand thanks go with thee.

HIPPOLITA   I have a suit to you,
  I must not have you weep when I am gone.   *Exit* [HIPPOLITA]

EUGENIA
  No, if I do, ne'er trust me. Easy fool!   220
  Thou hast put thyself into my power forever;
  Take heed of angering of me. I conceal!
  I feign a funeral! I keep my husband!
  'Las, I have been thinking any time these two years,
  I have kept him too long already.   225
  I'll go count o'er my suitors, that's my business,
  And prick the man down. I ha' six months to do it,
  But could dispatch him in one, were I put to it.
  Exit [EUGENIA]

227 *prick* choose by indicating with a sharp instrument;
also, of course, a bawdy pun.

Act III, scene i

Enter [GNOTHO] *the clown and* [*parish*] *clerk*

GNOTHO
You have searched o'er the parish chronicle, sir?

CLERK
  Yes, sir, I have found out the true age and date of the
  party you wot on.

GNOTHO   Pray you be covered, sir.

CLERK   When you have showed me the way, sir.   5

GNOTHO   Oh, sir, remember yourself, you are a clerk.

CLERK   A small clerk, sir.

GNOTHO
  Likely to be the wiser man, sir, for your greatest clerks
  are not always so, as 'tis reported.

CLERK   You are a great man in the parish, sir.   10

GNOTHO
  I understand myself so much the better, sir, for all the
  best in the parish pay duties to the clerk, and I would
  own you none, sir.

CLERK
  Since you'll have it so, I'll be the first to hide my head.
                    [*Puts on his hat.*]

GNOTHO
  Mine is a capcase. Now, to our business in your hand; 15
  Good luck, I hope, I long to be resolved.

CLERK
  Look you, sir, this is that cannot deceive you, this is
  the dial that goes ever true. You may say *ipse dixit*

3 *wot on*   inquired about
4 *Pray . . . sir.* 'Please put on your hat.'
12 *duties*   monies for the services of the Church (*Obs.*)
15 *Mine is a capcase.* 'Mine is in my travel-bag.'
18 *dial*   indicator; compass
18 *ipse dixit* authority speaks; he himself has spoken

upon this witness, and 'tis good in law too.

GNOTHO   Pray you, let's hear what it speaks.   20

CLERK
  Mark, sir: [*Reads*] *Agatha, the daughter of Pollux,*(this
  is your wife's name and the name of her father), *born* -

GNOTHO   Whose daughter say you?

CLERK   The daughter of Pollux.

GNOTHO   I take it his name was Bollux.*   25

CLERK
  P O L L U X the orthography, I assure you, sir, the
  word is corrupted else.

GNOTHO   Well, on, sir, of Pollux; now come on Castor.

CLERK
  Born in an. 1540, and now 'tis '99.* By this infallible
  record, sir, let me see, she is now just fifty-nine   30
  and wants but one.

GNOTHO   I am sorry she wants so much.

CLERK   Why, sir? Alas, 'tis nothing, 'tis but so
  many months, so many weeks, so many -

GNOTHO
  Do not deduct it to days, 'twill be the more tedious, 35
  and to measure it by hour-glasses were intolerable.

CLERK   Do not think on it, sir, half the time goes
  away in sleep; 'tis half the year in nights.

19 *witness* testimony
21 *Pollux* the first star of Gemini; one of the twin sons of
Tyndarus and Leda (see 1.28)
25 *Bollux* ME *ballock[s]*; testicles
26 *orthography* spelling
28 *Castor* the second star of Gemini

GNOTHO
  Oh, you mistake me, neighbour, I am loath to leave
  the good old woman. If she were gone now it would   40
  not grieve me, for what is a year, alas, but a ling-
  ering torment? And were it not better she were out
  of her pain? It must needs be a grief to us both.

CLERK   I would I knew how to ease you, neighbour.

GNOTHO   You speak kindly, truly, and if you say but   45
  Amen to it, which is a word that I know you are
  perfect in, it might be done. Clerks are the most
  indifferent honest men, for to the marriage of your
  enemy, or the burial of your friend, the curses or
  the blessings to you are all one; you say Amen to   50
  all.

CLERK   With a better will to the one than the other,
  neighbour, but I shall be glad to say Amen to anything might do you a pleasure.

GNOTHO   There is, first, something above your duty   55
  [*Gives him money*]. Now I would have you set forward the clock a little, to help the old woman out
  of her pain.

CLERK   I will speak to the sexton for that, but the
  day will go ne'er the faster for that.   60

GNOTHO   Oh, neighbour, you do not conceit me; not the
  jack of the clock-house, the hand of the dial, I
  mean. Come, I know you, being a great clerk, cannot
  choose but have the art to cast a figure.

CLERK   Never indeed, neighbour, I never had the   65
  judgment to cast a figure.

57 *to help* ed. (in to help Q)
59 *sexton* in church officer whose duties include bell-
ringing
61 *conceit* conceive; understand
62 *jack of the clock-house* a man or a mechanical device
which strikes the bell on the outside of the clock
62 *hand of the dial* 'the script in the birth registry'
(see above l. 18n)
66 *to cast a figure* to calculate astrologically (OED 39);
here, 'to arrange numbers'

GNOTHO   I'll show you on the backside of your book.
Look you, what figure's this?

CLERK   Four with a cipher, that's forty.

GNOTHO   So, forty; what's this now?   70

CLERK   The cipher is turned into 9 by adding the tail,
which makes forty-nine.

GNOTHO   Very well understood. What is it now?

CLERK   The 4 is turned into 3, 'tis now thirty-nine.

GNOTHO   Very well understood, and can you do this   75
again?

CLERK   Oh, easily, sir.

GNOTHO   A wager of that! Let me see the place of my
wife's age again.

CLERK   Look you, sir, 'tis here, 1540.   80

GNOTHO   Forty drachmas, you do not turn that forty
into thirty-nine.

CLERK   A match with you!

GNOTHO   Done! And you shall keep [the] stakes
yourself, there they are. [*Hands him money*]   85

CLERK   A firm match! But, stay sir, now I consider
it, I shall add a year to your wife's age. Let me
see, *Scirophorion* the 17, and now 'tis *Hecatombaion*
the 11. If I alter this, your wife will have but a
month to live by the law.   90

GNOTHO   That's all one, sir, either do it or pay me
my wager.

81 *drachmas* the principal monetary unit of Greece
88 *Scirophorion* ed. (Scirophon Q) the Athenian month beginning with the first new moon after the summer solstice
88 *Hecatombaeon* ed. (Hecatomcaon Q) the month preceding
Scirophorion

CLERK   Will you lose your wife before you lose your wager?

GNOTHO   A man may get two wives before half so much
  money by 'em. Will you do't?   95

CLERK   I hope you will conceal me, for 'tis flat
  corruption.

GNOTHO   Nay, sir, I would have you keep counsel for
  I lose my money by it, and should be laughed at for
  my labour if it should be known.   100

CLERK   Well, sir, there! 'Tis done, as perfect   39
  as can be found in black and white.* But, mum,
  sir, there's danger in this figure casting.

GNOTHO   Aye, sir, I know that better men than you
  have been thrown over the bar for as little. The   105
  best is, you can be but thrown out of the belfry.
  Enter the Cook, the Tailor, [the] Bailiff, and Butler

CLERK   Look close, here comes company. Asses have
  ears as well as pitchers.*

COOK   Oh, Gnotho, how is it? Here's a trick of dis-
  carded cards of us; we were ranked with coats as   110
  long as our old master lived.*

GNOTHO   And is this then the end of serving men?*

COOK   Yes, faith, this is the end of serving men. A
  wise man were better serve one God than all the men
  in the world.   115

GNOTHO   'Twas well spoke of a cook. And are all
  fallen into fasting days and ember weeks, that cooks
  are out of use?

96 *conceal me* 'keep secret'
105 *thrown over the bar* deprived of a status of a bar-
rister; disbarred (*Obs.* OED); perhaps arraigned
106 *thrown out of the belfry* lose a church position
116 *spoke of* spoken for
117 *fasting days* days of abstinence as religious obser-
vance
117 *ember weeks* the weeks in which ember days of fasting

TAILOR   And all tailors will be cut into lists and
shreds. If this world hold, we shall grow both out   120
of request.

BUTLER   And why not butlers as well as tailors? If
they can go naked, let 'em neither eat nor drink.

CLERK   That's strange, methinks, a lord should turn
away his tailor of all men. And how dost thou,   125
tailor?

TAILOR   I do so so. But, indeed, all our wants are
long of this publican, my lord's bailiff, for had he
been rent-gatherer still, our places had held together that are now seam-rent, nay, cracked in the   130
whole piece.

BAILIFF   Sir, if my lord had not sold his lands that
claim his rents, I should still have been the rent-
gatherer.

COOK   The truth is, except the coachman and the   135
footman, all serving men are out of request.

GNOTHO   Nay, say not so, for you were never in more
request than now, for requesting is but a kind of
begging; for when you say, "I beseech your worship's
charity," 'tis all one if you say I request it, and,   140
in that kind of requesting, I am sure serving men
were never in more request.

COOK   Troth, he says true. Well, let that pass, we
are upon a better adventure. I see, Gnotho, you
have been before us; we came to deal with this mer-   145
chant for some commodities.

and prayer occur. Ember days are the Wednesday, Friday,
and Saturday following (1) the first Sunday in Lent, (2)
Whitsunday, (3) Holy Cross Day, 14 Sept., (4) St. Lucia's
Day, 13 Dec. (OED)
119-20 *lists and shreds* strips and scraps
120-1 *grow both out of request* 'both be out of fashion'
127 *so so* pun on *sew sew*   128 *publican* collector
129-30 *together* ed. (together still Q)
130 *seam-rent* torn at the binding
130-1 *cracked in the whole piece* ripped completely apart

CLERK   With me, sir? Anything that I can.

BUTLER   Nay, we have looked out our wives already.
  Marry, to you we come to know the prices; that is,
  to know their ages; for so much reverence we bear   150
  to age, that the more aged they shall be the more
  dear to us.

TAILOR   The truth is, every man has laid by his widow;
  so they be lame enough, blind enough, and old [enough],
  'tis good enough.   155

CLERK   I keep the town stock. If you can but name 'em,
  I can tell their ages to-day.

ALL   We can tell their fortunes to an hour then.

CLERK   Only you must pay for turning of the leaves.
  [*They pass over the money*]

COOK   Oh, bountifully! Come, mine first!   160

BUTLER   The butler before the cook, while you live;
  there's few that eat before they drink in a morning.

TAILOR   Nay, then the tailor puts in his needle of
  priority, for men do clothe themselves before they
  either drink or eat.   165

BAILIFF   I will strive for no place. The longer e'er
  I marry my wife, the older she will be, and nearer
  her end and my ends.

CLERK   [*Continuing to write names from the church-book*]
  I will serve you all, gentlemen, if you will have
  patience.   170

GNOTHO   I commend your modesty, sir, you are a
  bailiff whose place is to come behind other men, as
  it were, in the bum of all the rest.

BAILIFF   So, sir, and you were about this business
  too, seeking out for a widow?   175

156 *stock* record of inhabitants

GNOTHO   Alack! No, sir, I am a married man and have
those cares upon me that you would fain run into.

BAILIFF   What, an old rich wife? Any man in this age
desires such a care.

GNOTHO   Troth, sir, I'll put a venture with you, if   180
you will. I have a lusty old queen to my wife, sound
of wind and limb, yet I'll give out to take three for
one at the marriage of my second wife.

BAILIFF   Aye, sir, but how near is she to the law?

GNOTHO   Take that at hazard, sir, there must be time,   185
you know, to get a new. Unsight, unseen, I take three
to one.

BAILIFF   Two to one I'll give, if she have but two
teeth in her head.

GNOTHO   A match! There's five drachmas for ten at   190
my next wife.

BAILIFF   A match! [*The parish clerk passes out name-
slips*]

COOK   I shall be fitted bravely, fifty-eight and
upwards 'tis but a year and a half, and I may chance
make friends and beg a year of the duke.   195

BUTLER   Hey, boys, I am made sir butler! My wife that
shall be wants but two months of her time. It shall
be one ere I marry her, and then the next will be a
honeymoon.

TAILOR   I outstrip you all! I shall have but six   200
weeks of Lent if I get my widow, and then comes
eating-tide, plump and gorgeous.

GNOTHO   This tailor will be a man if ever there were
any.

176 *fain* gladly
185 *at hazard* on chance
193 *bravely* handsomely

BAILIFF Now comes my turn. I hope, goodman, Finis, 205
  [*Addressing the last name-slip*] you that are still
  at the end of all with a "so be it." Well now, sirs,
  do you venture there as I have done, and I'll venture
  here after you. Good luck, I beseech thee!

CLERK Amen, sir.   210

BAILIFF That deserves a fee already [*Gives him
  money*]. There 'tis. Please me and have a better.

CLERK Amen, sir.

COOK How, two for one at your next wife? Is the old
  one living?   215

GNOTHO You have a fair match, I offer you no foul one.
  If death make not haste to call her, she'll make
  none to go to him.

BUTLER I know her, she's a lusty woman. I'll take
  the venture.   220

GNOTHO There's five drachmas for ten at my next wife.

BUTLER A bargain.

COOK Nay, then we'll be all merchants, give me.

TAILOR And me.

BUTLER What, has the bailiff sped?   225

BAILIFF I am content, but none of you shall know my
  happiness.

CLERK As well as any of you all, believe it, sir.

BAILIFF Oh, clerk, you are to speak last always.

CLERK I'll remember it hereafter, sir. You have   230
  done with me, gentlemen? *Enter* [GNOTHO'S] *wife,*
  [AGATHA]

ALL For this time, honest register.

232 *register* registrar

CLERK   Fare you well then; if you do, I'll cry Amen
to it.   Exit [CLERK]

COOK   Look you, sir, is not this your wife?   235

GNOTHO   My first wife, sir.

BUTLER   Nay, then we have made a good match on it.
If she have no forward disease, the woman may live
this dozen years by her age.

TAILOR   I'm afraid she's broken-winded, she holds   240
silence so long.

COOK   We'll now leave our venture to the event,   I
must a-wooing.

BUTLER   I'll but buy me a new dagger and overtake you.

BAILIFF   So we must all, for he that goes a-wooing to 245
a widow without a weapon, will never get her.   *Exeunt*
[*Manet* GNOTHO *and* AGATHA]

GNOTHO   Oh wife, wife!

AGATHA   What ails you, man, you speak so passionately?

GNOTHO   'Tis for thy sake, sweet wife. Who would
think so lusty an old woman, with reasonable good   250
teeth, and her tongue in as perfect use as ever it
was, should be so near her time? But the fates will
have it so.

AGATHA   What's the matter, man? You do amaze me.

GNOTHO   Thou art not sick neither, I warrant thee.   255

AGATHA   Not that I know of, sure.

GNOTHO   What pity 'tis, a woman should be so near
her end and yet not sick.

AGATHA   Near her end, man! Tush, I can guess at that,
I have years good yet of life in the remainder. I   260

238 *forward* progressive
248 *ails* ed. (ail Q)

want two yet, at least, of the full number; then the
law, I know, craves impotent and useless and not the
able women.

GNOTHO　　Aye, alas! I see thou hast been repairing
time as well as thou could'st; the old wrinkles are　265
well filled up, but the vermilion is seen too thick,
too thick, and I read what's written in thy forehead.
It agrees with the church-book

AGATHA　　Have you sought my age, man? And, I prithee,
how is it?　　　　　　　　　　　　　　　　　　　270

GNOTHO　　I shall but discomfort thee.

AGATHA　　Not at all, man, when there's no remedy, I
will go, though unwillingly.

GNOTHO　　1539. Thus it agrees with the book, you have
about a year to prepare yourself.　　　　　　　　275

AGATHA　　Out, alas! I hope there's more than so. But
do you not think a reprieve might be gotten for half
a score? And 'twere but five year[s], I would not
care; an able woman methinks, were to be pitied.

GNOTHO　　Aye, to be pitied, but not helped, no hope of　280
that; for, indeed, women have so blemished their own
reputations now-a-days, that it is thought the law
will meet them at fifty very shortly.

AGATHA　　Marry, the heavens forbid!

GNOTHO　　There's so many of you that when you are old　285
become witches: some profess physic and kill good
subjects faster than a burning fever; and then
schoolmistresses of sweet sin, which commonly we call
bawds, innumerable of that sort; for these and such
causes 'tis thought they shall not live above fifty.　290

AGATHA　　Aye, man, but this hurts not the good old women.

264-5 *repairing time*　attempting to cover up signs of age
266 *vermillion*　a red cosmetic
274 *Thus* ed. (Just Q)
286 *profess physic*　'claim to be doctors'

GNOTHO   Aye, faith, you are so like one another that a
man cannot distinguish 'em now. Were I an old woman,
I would desire to go before my time, and offer myself
willingly two or three years before. Oh, those are   295
brave women and worthy to be commended of all men in
the world, that when their husbands die run to be
burnt to death with 'em. There's honour and credit;
give me half a dozen such wives!

AGATHA   Aye, if her husband were dead before, 'twere   300
a reasonable request. If you were dead, I could be
content to be so.

GNOTHO   Fie, that's not likely, for thou had'st two
husbands before me.

AGATHA   Thou would'st not have me die, would'st thou, 305
husband?

GNOTHO   No, I do not speak to that purpose, but I say
what credit it were for me and thee if thou would'st,
then thou should'st never be suspected for a witch,
a physician, a bawd, or any of those things, and   310
then how daintily should I mourn for thee, how bravely
should I see thee buried. When, alas, if he goes
before, it cannot choose but be a great grief to him
to think he has not seen his wife well buried. There
be such virtuous women in the world, but too few,   315
who desire to die seven years before their time with
all their hearts.

AGATHA   I have not the heart to be of that mind.
But, indeed, husband, I think you would have me
gone.   320

GNOTHO   No, alas! I speak but for your good and your
credit, for when a woman may die quickly, why should
she go to law for her death? Alack! I need not wish
thee gone for thou hast but a short time to stay with
me; you do not know how near 'tis. It must out, you 325
have but a month to live by the law.

AGATHA   Out, alas!

297 *run* ed. (they run Q)

GNOTHO   Nay, scarce so much.

AGATHA   On, oh, oh, my heart! *[She] swoons*

GNOTHO   Aye, so, if thou would'st go away quietly,   330
     'twere sweetly done and like a kind wife. Lie but
     a little longer and the bell shall toll for thee.

AGATHA   Oh, my heart, but a month to live!

GNOTHO   *[Aside]*
     Alas, why would'st thou come back again for a month?
     I'll throw her down again. *[Leans over her]* Oh,   335
     woman, 'tis not three weeks, I think a fortnight is
     the most.

AGATHA   Nay, then, I am gone already. *Swoons [again]*

GNOTHO   I would make haste to the sexton now, but I'm
     afraid the tolling of the bell will wake her again.   340
     If she be so wise as to go now - she stirs again,
     there's two lives of the nine gone.

AGATHA   Oh, would'st not thou help to recover me,
     husband?

GNOTHO   Alas, I could not find in my heart to hold   345
     thee by thy nose, or box thy cheeks, it goes against
     my conscience.

AGATHA   I will not be thus frighted to my death,
     I'll search the church record a fortnight;
     'Tis too little conscience, I cannot be so near.   350
     Oh time, if thou be'est kind, lend me but a year.
                                        Exit[AGATHA]

GNOTHO   What a spite's this, that a man cannot
     persuade his wife to die in any time with her good
     will. I have another bespoke already. Though a
     piece of old beef will serve to breakfast, yet a   355
     man would be glad of a chicken to supper. The

332 *bell* death bell
342 *there's two . . . gone.* 1732 Fuller, *Gnomologia* p. 2,
A cat has nine lives, a woman has nine cats' lives. (see
also *R. J.* III.i.80-1)
352 *spite's* rancour's

The clerk, I hope, understands no Hebrew and cannot
write backward what he hath writ forward already,*
and then I am well enough.
'Tis but a month at most, if that were gone　　　360
My venture comes in with her two for one.
'Tis use enough, a conscience for a broker –
If he had a conscience.

362 *broker* ed. (brother Q)

Act III, scene ii

Enter EUGENIA *at one door,* SIMONIDES, *Courtiers, at the other.*

EUGENIA   Gentlemen courtiers.

1 COURTIER   [*Bowing extravagantly*]
  All your servants vowed, lady.

EUGENIA
  Oh, I shall kill myself with infinite laughter!
  Will nobody take my part?

SIMONIDES   And it be a laughing business,   5
  Put it to me, I'm one of the best in Europe.
  My father died last too, I have the most cause.

EUGENIA
  You have picked out such a time, sweet gentlemen,
  To make your spleen a banquet.

SIMONIDES   Oh the jest, lady!   10
  I have a jaw stands ready for it, I'll gape
  Half way and meet it.

EUGENIA   My old husband,
  That cannot say his prayers out for jealousy
  And madness, at your coming first to woo me –   15

SIMONIDES   Well said!

1 COURTIER   Go on!

2 COURTIER   On, on!

EUGENIA   Takes counsel with the secrets of all art
  To make himself youthful again.   20

SIMONIDES   How? Youthful! ha, ha, ha.

8 *have* ed. (ha Q)
9 *To make your spleen a banquet* 'to feast your desire for
merriment'
11 *jaw* mouth

EUGENIA
A man of forty-five he would feign seem to be,
Or scarce so much, if he might have his will indeed.

SIMONIDES
Aye, but his white hairs, they'll betray his hoariness.

EUGENIA
Why, there you are wide, he's not the man you take
                                  him for;   25
Nor will you know him when you see him again,
There will be five to one laid upon that.

1 COURTIER   How?

EUGENIA   Nay, you did well to laugh faintly there.
I promise you, I think he'll outlive me now   30
And deceive law and all.

SIMONIDES   Marry, gout forbid!

EUGENIA   You little think he was at fencing school
At four o'clock this morning.

SIMONIDES   How, at fencing school?   35

EUGENIA   Else give no trust to woman.

SIMONIDES   By this light
I do not like him, then; he's like to live
Longer than I, for he may kill me first, now.

EUGENIA   His dancer now came in, as I met you.   40

1 COURTIER   His dancer, too?

EUGENIA   They observe turns and hours with him;
The great French rider will be here at ten
With his curvetting horse.

2 COURTIER   These notwithstanding,   45

26 *Nor* ed. (Nay Q)
32 *gout* a specific constitutional disease; a dialectal
pronunciation for God
44 *curvetting* prancing

His hair and wrinkles will betray his age.

EUGENIA
  I'm sure his head and beard, as he has ordered it,
  Looks not past fifty now. He'll bring it to forty
  Within these four days, for nine times an hour at least
  He takes a black lead comb and kembs it over.   50
  Three-quarters of his beard is under fifty;
  There's but a little tuft of fourscore left
  All of one side which will be black by Monday. *Enter*
  LISANDER
  And to approve my truth, see where he comes?
  Laugh softly, gentlemen, and look upon him. [*They*   55
  hide]

SIMONIDES
  Now, by this hand, he's almost black in the mouth
                                        indeed.

1 COURTIER   He should die shortly, then.

SIMONIDES   Marry, methinks he dies too fast already,
  For he was all white but a week ago.

1 COURTIER
  Oh, this same coney-white takes an excellent black   60
  Too soon. A mischief on it!

2 COURTIER   He will beguile us all
  If that little tuft northward turn black too.

EUGENIA   Nay, sir, I wonder 'tis so long a-turning.

SIMONIDES
  Maybe some fairy's child, held forth at midnight,   65
  Has pissed upon that side.

1 COURTIER   Is this the beard?

LISANDER   [*Struts about the stage, talking to himself*]
  Ah, sirrah. My young boys, I shall be for you. [*Looks
  into a mirror*]

50 *kembs* combs *(dial.)*
58 *dies* Pun; expires; changes colour
60 *coney-white* white rabbit

This little mangey tuft takes up more time
Than all the beard beside! - Come you a-wooing   70
And I alive and lusty?   You shall find
An alteration, Jack-boys, I have a spirit yet -
[Again lifts the mirror]
And I could match my hair to it, there's the fault, -
And can do offices of youth yet lightly.
At least I will do, though it pain me a little.   75
Shall not a man for a little foolish age
Enjoy his wife to himself?   Must young court tits
Play tomboy's tricks with her and he live, ha?
I have blood that will not bear it, - *[Pauses discon-*
consolately]   yet, I confess,
I should be at my prayers.   But! Where's the dancer
                                             there?   80
Ent[er] Dan[cing Master]

DANCING MASTER   Here, sir.

LISANDER   Come, come, come, one trick a day
And I shall soon recover all again.

EUGENIA   *[Whispering]*
'Slight, and you laugh too loud, we are all discovered,
                                          gentlemen.

SIMONIDES
And I have a scurvy ginny laugh o' mine own   85
Will spoil all, I'm afraid.

EUGENIA   Marry, take heed, sir.

SIMONIDES
Nay, and I should be hanged, I can't leave it.
Pup! There 'tis. *[Bursts out laughing]*

72 *Jack-boys* grooms, stable-boys
82 *trick* feat
83 *recover* regain skill
84 *'slight* a petty oath; abbreviation for God's light
85 *scurvy* scurfy (vb. to scurf: to rise to the surface);
rising
85 *ginny laugh* a Jenny laugh, a girl's laugh, high-pitched;
or, perhaps, a 'ginning (beginning) laugh; (*grinning* Dyce,
Gifford, Bullen)
85 *o'* ed. (a Q)

EUGENIA   Peace! Oh, peace!   90

LISANDER   Come, I am ready, sir.
   I hear the church-book's lost where I was born too,
   And that shall set me back one-and-twenty years;
   There is no little comfort left in that.
   And, my three court codlings, that look parboiled,   95
   As if they came from Cupid's scalding house, -

SIMONIDES   He means me specially, I hold my life.

DANCING MASTER
   What trick will your old worship learn this morning, sir?

LISANDER   Marry, a trick? If thou couldst teach a man
   To keep his wife to himself, I'd fain learn that.   100

DANCING MASTER
   That's a hard trick for an old man specially,
   The horse-trick comes the nearest.

LISANDER   Thou sayest true, i'faith,
   They must be horsed indeed, else there's no keeping
                                           on 'em, 105
   And horseplay at fourscore is not so ready.

DANCING MASTER   Look you, here's your worship's
   horse-trick, sir. [*Demonstrates by springing upwards.*]

LISANDER   Nay, say not so,
   'Tis none of mine; I fall down horse and man
   If I but offer at it.

DANCING MASTER   My life for yours, sir.   110

LISANDER   Sayest thou me so? [*Springs aloft*]

95 *codlings* a young or small cod; or, perhaps, quodling
(*Obs.*) figuratively applied to a raw youth
95 *parboiled* overheated
96 *Cupid's scalding house* a brothel
102 **horse**-*trick* a bawdy pun on executing a spring, horse-
like, to cover a mare
104 *horsed* of a mare: covered by a horse (*Obs.* OED)

DANCING MASTER   Well offered, by my viol, sir.

LISANDER
    A pox of this horse-trick, it has played the jade
                                              with me
    And given me a wrench in the back.

DANCING MASTER
    Now, here's your inturn, and your trick above
                                ground.   115

LISANDER
    Prithee, no more, unless thou hast a mind
    To lay me underground. One of these tricks
    Is enough in a morning.

DANCING MASTER   For your galliare, sir,
    You are complete enough. Aye, and may challenge   120
    The proudest coxcomb of 'em all, I'll stand to it.

LISANDER
    Faith, and I've other weapons for the rest too.
    I have prepared for 'em, if e'er I take
    My Gregories here again.

SIMONIDES
    Oh, I shall burst, I can hold out no longer.
                            [*Laughs loudly*]   125

EUGENIA   He spoils all.   [*They come forward*]

LISANDER
    The devil and his grinners! Are you come?
    Bring forth the weapons, we shall find you play!
    All feats of youth too, Jack-boys, feats of youth,
    And these weapons: drinking, fencing, dancing.   130

112 *viol* a bowed instrument, similar to the violin, common
in the 16th and 17th centuries
113 *jade* to make a jade of (a horse); to exhaust
119 *galliard* a quick and lively dance in triple time (*Hist.*
OED)
121 *coxcomb* a conceited youth; a princos
124 *Gregories* gallants

Your own road waits you, glisterpipes. I'm old, you say?
Yes, parlous old, kids, and you mark me well;
This beard cannot get children, you lank suck-eggs,
Unless such weasels come from court to help us?
We will get our own brats, you lecherous dog-bolts.   135
Well said, down with 'em, now we shall see your spirits.
Enter [servants] with [foils, caraffes, and] glasses.
[The courtiers draw back.]
What, dwindle you already?

2 COURTIER   I have no quality.

SIMONIDES
Nor I, unless drinking may be reckoned for one.

1 COURTIER   Why, Sim, it shall.   140

LISANDER   Come, dare you choose your weapon now?

1 COURTIER   I? Dancing, sir, and you will be so hasty.

LISANDER   We're for you, sir.

2 COURTIER   Fencing, I.

LISANDER   We'll answer you too.   145

SIMONIDES   I'm for drinking, your wet weapon there.

LISANDER
That wet one has cost many a princox' life,
And I will send it through you with a powder.

SIMONIDES
Let come with a pox, I care not so it be drink.

131 *waits* ed. (waies Q) 131 *glisterpipes* clysterpipes,
tubes or pipes for administrating enemas
132 *parlous* dangerously cunning
133 *suck-eggs* animals purported to suck eggs, e.g. a
weasel, a cuckoo; hence, one who would invade another man's
nest
135 *dog-bolts* generally a contemptible fellow, perhaps
originating in a 'mere tool to be put to any use' (OED)
147 *princox'* a saucy fellow; a coxcomb 148 *powder* gun-
powder, an explosive; a dose of medicine, a laxative
149 *pox* an eruption, perhaps associated with syphilis

I hope my guts will hold, and that's even all   150
A gentleman can look for of such trillibubs.

LISANDER
   Play the first weapon, come, strike, strike I say!
   Yes, yes, you shall be first; i'll observe court rules,
   Always the worst goes foremost, so 'twill prove, I hope.
   [*Music. The first courtier dances*] *a galliard*
   So, sir, you've spit your poison, now come I.   155
   [*Aside*] Now forty years ago backward and assist me,
   Fall from me half my age, but for three minutes
   That I may feel no crick! I will put fair for it
   Although I hazard twenty sciaticas.
   [*Again music. LISANDER dances a galliard*]
   So, I have hit you!   160

1 COURTIER   You've done well, i'faith, sir.

LISANDER   If you confess it well, 'tis excellent,
   And I have hit you soundly. I am warm now,
   The second weapon instantly.

2 COURTIER   What, so quick, sir?   165
   Will you not allow yourself a breathing time?

LISANDER
   I've breath enough at all times, Lucifer's muskcod,
   To give your perfumed worship three vennies.
   A sound old man puts his thrust better home
   Than a spiced young man. [*They fence*] There, aye!   170
   [*Makes the first hit*]

2 COURTIER   Then have at you, fourscore.

LISANDER
   You lie, twenty, I hope, and you shall find it.

151 *trillibubs* entrails (ref. cited in OED); "This seems to
be a cant word for anything of a trifling nature" Gifford.
s.d. *a galliard* ed. (a Galliear laminiard Q) "The word
Laminiard probably represents the name of the tune, perhaps
a corruption of 'La Mignarde'" Bullen
159 *sciaticas* pains caused by injury to the great sciatic
nerve
167 *Lucifer's muskcod* a scented fop (OED) of the devil
168 *vennies* hits or thrusts in fencing

SIMONIDES
I'm glad I missed this weapon. I ['d] had an eye
Popped out e'er this time, or my two butter teeth
Thrust down my throat instead of a flap-dragon.   175

LISANDER
There's two, pentweezle! *[Makes a second hit]*

DANCING MASTER   Excellently touched, sir.

2 COURTIER
Had ever man such luck? Speak your opinion, gentlemen.

SIMONIDES
Methinks your luck's good that your eyes are in still,
Mine would have dropped out like a pig's, half-
                                        roasted.   180

LISANDER
There wants a third, and there 'tis again! *[Makes
a third hit]*

2 COURTIER   The devil has steeled him.

EUGENIA   What a strong fiend is jealousy!

LISANDER   You're dispatched, bear-whelp!

SIMONIDES   Now comes my weapon in.   185

LISANDER   Here, toadstool, here!
'Tis with you I must play these three wet vennies.

SIMONIDES   Vennies in Venice glasses, let 'em come!
They'll bruise no flesh, I'm sure, nor break no bones.

1 COURTIER   Yet you may drink your eyes out, sir.   190

174 *butter teeth*   the front or incisor teeth; later buck
teeth (OED)
175 *flap-dragon*   a raisin caught out of burning brandy and
extinguished by closing the mouth over it (OED); (see also
LLL V.i 45)   176 *pentweezle*   penned weasel
187 *you I* ed. (you and I Q)
188 *Venice glasses*   goblets made from the delicate glass
originally manufactured at Murano, Italy

SIMONIDES
    Aye, but that's nothing, then they go voluntarily.
    I do not love to have 'em thrust out
    Whether they will or no.

LISANDER
    Here's your first weapon, duck's meat! *[Drinks and
    then passes a glass]*

SIMONIDES   How? A Dutch what-you-call-'em   195
    'Stead of a German faulchion? A shrewd weapon,
    And, of all things, hard to be taken down.
    Yet, down it must. *[Drinks]* I have a nose goes in
                                        to it;
    I shall drink double, I think.

1 COURTIER   The sooner off, Sim.   200

LISANDER
    I'll pay you speedily _____ _____, with a trick*
    I learned once amongst drunkards. Here's half pike.
                                    [Drinks again]

SIMONIDES
    Half pike comes well after Dutch what-you-call-'em,
    They'd never be asunder by their good will.

1 COURTIER   Well pulled of an old fellow!   205

LISANDER
    Oh, but your fellows pull better at a rope. *[Passes
    a second glass]*

1 COURTIER   There's a hair, Sim, in that glass.

194 *duck's meat* perhaps Proverbial; [1523] 1568 Skelton
How Doughty Duke Albany 1.222: *Wks.*, II 74: Syr duke, nay
syr ducke...for small lucke Ye haue in feates of warre
(*Tilley* D636); or, perhaps, duck as opposed to drake thus
implying a charge of effeminacy
195 *A Dutch what-you-call-'em* A Dutch widow, a harlot
196 *faulchion* a broad sword more or less curved with the
edge on the convex side (OED) 203 *pike* a weapon consisting
of a long shaft with a pointed head of iron or steel; a
penis   204 *asunder* put into a position apart; separate
206 *pull better at a rope* exert more influence
207 *hair* hare; to swallow a hare: to get exceedingly drunk

SIMONIDES
And it be as long as a halter, down it goes. *[Drinks]*
No hair shall cross me.

LISANDER
I'll make you stink worse than your polecats do.
                        [Drinks again]   210
Here's long-sword, your last weapon. *[Offers the
                                  third glass]*

SIMONIDES   No more weapons.

1 COURTIER
Why! How now, Sim? Bear up, thou shamest us all else.

SIMONIDES
['S]light, I shall shame you worse and I stay longer.
I ha' got the scotomy in my head already.
                        [Staggers about]   215
The whimsy, you all turn round! Do not you dance,
                              gallants?

2 COURTIER
Pish, what's all this? Why, Sim, look, the last venny.

SIMONIDES
No more vennies go down here, for these two are coming
                              up again.

2 COURTIER   Out! The disgrace of drinkers!

SIMONIDES   Yes, 'twill out.   220
Do you smell nothing yet?

1 COURTIER   Smell?

SIMONIDES
Farewell quickly, then, it will do if I stay. *Exit*
                           [SIMONIDES]

209 *no hair shall cross me* Proverbial; Erasmus *Adagia*,
693F: *Lepus apparens infortunatum facit erit* (see *Tilley*
H150)
210 *I'll* ed. (I Q)
215 *scotomy* dizziness accompanied by dimness of sight
218 *go* ed. (goes Q)

1 COURTIER   A foil go with thee!

LISANDER
  What! Shall we put down youth at her own virtues?   225
  Beat folly in her own ground? Wonderous much!
  Why may not we be held as full sufficient
  To love our own wives then, get our own children,
  And live in free peace 'till we be dissolved?
  For such spring butterflies that are gaudy-winged,   230
  But no more substance than those shamble-flies
  Which butcher's boys snap between sleep and waking,
  Come but to crush you once; you are all but maggots
  For all your beamy outsides! *Enter* CLEANTHES

EUGENIA   Here's Cleanthes,   235
  He comes to chide. Let him alone a little;
  Our cause will be revenged. Look, look, his face
  Is set for stormy weather. Do but mark
  How the clouds gather in it; 'twill pour down straight.

CLEANTHES   [*To* LISANDER]
  Methinks I partly know you, that's my grief.   240
  Could you all be lost, that had been handsome;
  But to be known at all, 'tis more than shameful!
  Why, was not your name wont to be Lisander?

LISANDER   'Tis so still, coz.

CLEANTHES
  Judgment, defer thy coming! Else this man's
                              miserable.   245

EUGENIA   I told you there would be a shower anon.

2 COURTIER
  We'll in and hide our noddles. *Exeunt Courtiers and*
                                         EUGENIA

CLEANTHES   What devil brought this colour to your mind,
  Which since my childhood I ne'er saw you wear?
  You were ever of an innocent gloss   250

_____

224 *foil* disgrace (*Obs.* OED); also a pun on a fencing
weapon
241 *Could you all* ed. (Could you not all Q)
249 *my* ed. (your Q)

Since I was ripe for knowledge; and would you lose it
And change the livery of saints and angels
For this mixed monstrousness! To force a ground
That has been so long hallowed like a temple,
To bring forth fruits of earth now, and turn black   255
To the wild cries of lust and the complexion
Of sin in act, lost and long since repented!
Would you begin a work ne'er yet attempted,
To pull time backward?
See what your wife will do! Are your wits perfect?   260

LISANDER   My wits!

CLEANTHES
I like it ten times worse; for it had been safer
Now to be mad, and more excusable!
I hear you dance again, and do strange follies.

LISANDER
I must confess I have been put to some, coz.   265

CLEANTHES   And yet you are not mad? Pray, say not so,
Give me that comfort of you that you are mad,
That I may think you are at worst. For, if
You are not mad, I then must guess you have
The first of some disease was never heard of,   270
Which may be worse than madness, and more fearful.
You'd weep to see yourself else, and your care
To pray would quickly turn you white again.
I had a father, had he lived his month out,
But to have seen this most prodigious folly,   275
There needed not the law to have cut him off;
The sight of this had proved his executioner,
And broke his heart. He would have held it equal
Done to a sanctuary! For what is age
But the holy place of life, chapel of ease   280
For all men's wearied miseries; and, to rob
That of her ornament, it is accursed,
As from a priest to steal a holy vestment;
Aye, and convert it to a sinful covering. *Exit* LISANDER
I see it has done him good; blessing go with it,   285

255 *black* Q (*back* Bullen) an obvious reference to
Lisander's dying of his hair and beard; perhaps an allusion
to the Proverb: as black as the devil (*Tilley* D217)
275 *have* ed. (ha Q)

Such as may make him pure again. *Enter* EUGENIA

EUGENIA   'Twas bravely touched, i'faith, sir.

CLEANTHES   Oh, you're welcome.

EUGENIA   Exceedingly well handled.

CLEANTHES   'Tis to you I come; he fell but in my way. 290

EUGENIA   You marked his beard, cousin?

CLEANTHES   Mark me.

EUGENIA   Did you ever see a hair so changed?

CLEANTHES   [*Aside*]
I must be forced to wake her loudly too;
The devil has rocked her so fast asleep.   295
[*Turns on* EUGENIA] Strumpet!

EUGENIA   Do you call, sir?

CLEANTHES   Whore!

EUGENIA   How do you, sir?

CLEANTHES   Be I ne'er so well   300
I must be sick of thee! Thou art a disease
That stickest to the heart, as all such women are.

EUGENIA   What ails our kindred?

CLEANTHES   Bless me, she sleeps still!
What a dead modesty is in this woman!   305
Will never blush again? Look on thy work
But with a Christian eye, 'twould turn thy heart
Into a shower of blood to be the cause
Of that old man's destruction. Think upon it!
Ruin eternally! For through thy loose follies   310
Heaven has found him a faint servant lately.
His goodness had gone backward and engendered
With his old sins again, has lost his prayers,
And all the tears that were companions with 'em;

312 *engendered* coupled

And, like a blindfold man, giddy and blinded,   315
Thinking he goes right on still, swerves but one foot
And turns to the same place where he set out.
So he, that took his farewell of the world
And cast the joys behind him out of sight,
Summed up his hours, made even with time and men,   320
Is now in heart arrived at youth again,
All by thy wildness. Thy too hasty lust
Has driven him to this strong apostacy.
Immodesty like thine was never equalled!
I've heard of women, shall I call 'em so,   325
Have welcomed suitors e'er the corps' were cold,
But thou! Thy husband['s] living! Thou art too bold!

EUGENIA   Well, have you done now, sir?

CLEANTHES   Look, look, she smiles yet!

EUGENIA   All this is nothing to a mind resolved;   330
Ask any woman that, she'll tell you so much.
You have only shown a pretty saucy wit
Which I shall not forget, nor to requite it
You shall hear from me shortly.

CLEANTHES   Shameless woman!
I take my counsel from thee, 'tis too honest,
And leave thee wholly to thy stronger master.
Bless the sex of thee from thee! That's my prayer.
Were all like thee, so impudently common,
No man would be found to wed a woman. *Exit*
                              [CLEANTHES]   340

EUGENIA   I'll fit you gloriously!
He that attempts to take away my pleasure,
I'll take away his joy, and I can, sure.
His concealed father pays for it! I'll even tell
Him that I mean to make my husband next *Enter*
                              SIMONIDES   345
And he shall tell the duke. Mass! here he comes.

SIMONIDES   Has had a bout with me too.

323 *apostacy* abandonment of moral principles
341 *fit* match; or, perhaps, a var. (dial. or vulgar) of
fight

EUGENIA   What! No! Since, sir?

SIMONIDES
  A flirt, a little flirt; he called me strange names,
  But I ne'er minded him.   350

EUGENIA   You shall quit him, sir,
  When he as little minds you.

SIMONIDES   I like that well.
  I love to be revenged when no one thinks of me,
  There's little danger that way.   355

EUGENIA   This is it then:
  He you shall strike, your stroke shall be profound,
  And yet your foe not guess who gave the wound.

SIMONIDES
  By my troth, I love to give such wounds.   *Exeunt [omnes]*

349 *flirt* trifle
359 *By* ed. (A Q)

Act IV, scene i

Enter [GNOTHO, *the*] *Clown, Butler, Bailiff, Tailor*
Cook, Drawer, [*and* SIREN, *the*] *Wench.*

DRAWER   Welcome, gentlemen, will you not draw
near? Will you drink at door, gentlemen?

BUTLER   Oh, the summer air's best!

DRAWER   What wine will [it] please you drink,
gentlemen?   5

BUTLER   De Clare, sirrah.   [*Exit Drawer*]

GNOTHO   What! You're all sped already, bullies?

COOK   My widow's on the spit and half ready, lad.   A
turn or two more, and I have done with her.

GNOTHO   Then, Cook, I hope you have basted her   10
before this time.

COOK   And stuck her with rosemary too, to
sweeten her, she was tainted ere she came
to my hands. What an old piece of flesh of
fifty-nine, eleven months and upwards! She   15
must needs be flyblown.*

GNOTHO   Put her off, put her off, though you
lose by her; the weather's hot.

COOK   Why, Drawer!   *Enter Drawer*

DRAWER   By and by! Here, gentlemen, here's the   20
quintessence of Greece, the sages never drunk
better grape.

COOK   Sir, the mad Greeks of this age can taste
their Palermo as well as the sage Greeks did

6 *De Clare* claret
7 *sped* successful (*arch.* OED I.1.); quick in dispatch (OED
11.10); discharged (*vulgar* OED II.10b)
24 *Palermo* a wine from Palermo in Sicily (*Obs.* OED)

before 'em. Fill, lick-spiggot.   25

DRAWER   *Ad imum,* sir.

GNOTHO   My friends, I must doubly invite you all,
   the fifth of the next month, to the funeral
   of my first wife and to the marriage of my second.
   My two to one, this is she!   30

COOK   I hope some of us will be ready for the
   funeral of our wives by that time to go with
   thee; but shall they be both of a day?

GNOTHO   Oh, best of all, sir! Where sorrow and
   joy meet together, one will help away with another   35
   the better. Besides, there will no charges saved
   too, the same rosemary that serves for the funeral,
   will serve for the wedding.

BUTLER   How long do you make account to be a
   widower, sir?   40

GNOTHO   Some half an hour; long enough for a
   conscience! Come, come, let's have some agility;
   is there no music in the house?

DRAWER   Yes, sir, here are sweet wire-drawers.

COOK   Oh, that makes them and you seldom a part;   45
   you are wine-drawers and they wire-drawers.

TAILOR   And both govern by the pegs too.

GNOTHO   And you have pipes in your consort too?

DRAWER   And sack butts too, sir.

25 *lick-spiggot* one who licks the tap of the wine cask
26 *ad imum* to the last
44 *wire-drawers* ed. (wire-drawers in the house Q)   one who
plays a stringed instrument (*Obs* ref. cited in OED)
47 *pegs* a wooden pin used as a vent in a wine cask, a
tuning pin of a stringed instrument
48 *consort* fellowship; also a pun on concert
49 *sack butts* casks of sherry; obsolete musical instruments

BUTLER   But the heads of your instruments differ;   50
your's are hogsheads, their[s] cittern and
gitternheads.*

BAILIFF   All wooden heads! There, they meet again.

COOK   Bid 'em strike up, we'll have a dance.
Gnotho, come, thou shall foot it too.   55
[*Exit Drawer*]

GNOTHO   No dancing with me, we have Siren here.

COOK   Siren! 'twas Hiren, the fair Greek, man.*

GNOTHO   Five drachmas of that! I say Siren,
the fair Greek, and so are all fair Greeks.

COOK   A match! Five drachmas her name was Hiren.   60

GNOTHO   Siren's name was Siren for five drachmas.

COOK   'Tis done.

TAILOR   Take heed what you do, Gnotho.

GNOTHO   Do not I know our own countrywomen?
Siren and Nell of Greece, two of the fairest   65
Greeks that ever were.

COOK   That Nell was Helen of Greece too.

GNOTHO   As long as she tarried with her husband,
she was Ellen; but after she came to Troy, she
was Nell of Troy, or Bonny Nell, whether you   70

51 *hogsheads* wooden casks holding 63 old wine gallons or
52 1/2 imperial gallons
51-52 *cittern and gittern* variant spellings for instruments of the guitar kind, but strung with wire, and played
with a plectrum or quill (OED)
55 *foot* ed. (foole Q)
69 *Ellen* alternate spelling for *ell*; a measure originally
designating the length of the forearm (ulna); in England
45 inches
70 *Nell* a nellen for an ellen (see above)

will or no.

TAILOR   Why? Did she grow shorter when she
came to Troy?

GNOTHO   She grew longer, if you mark the story.
when she grew to be an ell, she was deeper   75
than any yard of Troy could reach by a quarter.*
There was Cressid was Troy weight, and Nell
was haberdepoise, she held more by four ounces
than Cressida.

BAILIFF   They say she caused many wounds to be   80
given in Troy.

GNOTHO   True, she was wounded there herself and
cured again by plaster of Paris, and ever since
that has been used to stop holes with.*
Enter Drawer

DRAWER   Gentlemen, if you be disposed to be merry,   85
the music is ready to strike up and here's a
consort of mad Greeks. I know not whether
they be men or women, or between both, they
have what-you-call-'em[s], wizards, on their
faces.   90

COOK   Vizards, goodman lick-spiggot.

BUTLER   If they be wise women, they may be
wizards too.

DRAWER   They desire to enter amongst any merry
company of gentlemen goodfellows for a strain   95
or two.

COOK   We'll strain ourselves with 'em. Say let
'em come now, for the honour of Epire!

77 *Cressid was Troy weight* she weighed 12 ounces to the
pound
78 *haberdepoise* avoirdupois; thus Helen at 16 ounces to
the pound held 4 ounces more than Cressida who was only 12
ounces to the pound
89 *wizards* ed. (vizards Q)
97 *Say let . . . honour of Epire!* ed. (in the Q the word

[*Enter* GNOTHO'S *wife,* AGATHA,*and the old wives
of the others, masked.*]

GNOTHO　We have Siren here! She['s] dancing
with me. *The dance of old women masked;*　　　100
*then [they] offer to take [out] the men;
they agree all but* GNOTHO; *he sits with
his wench, after [the dance] they whisper.*

COOK　Aye, so kind! Then every one his wench
to his several room. Gnotho, we are all
provided now, as you are.
Exeunt each with his wife; manet GNOTHO'S *wife.*

GNOTHO
I shall have two, it seems. Away! I have Siren　　105
here already.

AGATHA　[*unmasks*]
What a mermaid!

GNOTHO
No, but a maid, horse-face. Oh, old woman, is it you?

AGATHA　Yes, 'tis I. All the rest have gulled
themselves and taken their own wives; and shall　　110
know that they have done more than they can
well answer. But, I pray you, husband, what
are you doing?

GNOTHO　Faith, thus should I do if thou wert
dead, old Ag, and thou hast not long to live,　　115
I'm sure. We have Siren here.

AGATHA　Art thou so shameless whilst I am living,
to keep one under my nose?

GNOTHO　No, Ag, I do prize her far above thy nose.
If thou would'st lay me both thine eyes in my　　120

Gnothoes appears between the two phrases of this sentence.
The name obviously belongs below to designate the next
speaker.)
107 *mermaid*　whore-maid
108 *horse-face*　whore's face

hand to boot, I'll not leave her. Art not ashamed
to be seen in a tavern, and hast scarce a fortnight
to live? Oh, old woman, what art thou! Must thou
find no time to think of thy end?

AGATHA   Oh, unkind villain!   125

GNOTHO   [*Turns to Siren*]
And then, sweetheart, thou shalt have two new gowns,
and the best of this old woman's shall make thee
raiments for the working days.

AGATHA   Oh, rascal! Dost thou quarter my clothes
already too?   130

GNOTHO   Her ruffs will serve thee for nothing but
to wash dishes, for thou shalt have nine of the
new fashion.

AGATHA   Impudent villain! Shameless harlot!

GNOTHO   You may hear she never wore any but rails   135
all her lifetime.

AGATHA   Let me come, I'll tear the strumpet from him!

GNOTHO   Dar'st thou call my wife strumpet, thou preter-
pluperfect tense of a woman? I'll make thee do penance
in the sheet thou shalt be buried in. Abuse my   140
choice, my two to one!

AGATHA   No, unkind villain, I'll deceive thee yet!
I have a reprieve for five years of life, I am with
child.

127 *old* ed. (old old Q)
129 *quarter* divide
131 *ruffs* articles of neckwear usually made of fluted linen
or muslin
135 *rails* nagging complaints; neckerchiefs or small shawls
(see 1592 Nashe *Pierce Pennilesse*, 1. 74)
139-40 *preter-pluperfect tense* grammatically, preterite;
humorously, more than perfectly past

SIREN   Cud, so, Gnotho, I'll not tarry so long!   145
  Five years! I may bury two husbands by that time.

GNOTHO   Alas, give the poor woman leave to talk.
  She with child? I with a puppy! As long as
  I have thee by me, she shall not be with child,
  I warrant thee.   150

AGATHA   The law and thou and all shall find I am
  with child.

GNOTHO   I'll take my corporal oath I begat it not,
  and then thou die'st for adultery.

AGATHA   No matter, that will ask some time in the   155
  proof.

GNOTHO   Oh, you'd be stoned to death, would you?*
  All old women would die o' that fashion with all
  their hearts, but the law shall overthrow you
  the t'other way first.   160

SIREN   Indeed, if it be so, I will not linger
  so long, Gnotho.

GNOTHO   Away, away, some botcher has got it;
  'tis but a cushion, I warrant thee. The old
  woman is loath to depart; she never sung other   165
  tune in her life.

SIREN   We will not have our noses bored with a
  cushion if it be so.

GNOTHO   Go, go thy ways, thou old almanac at the
  twenty-eighth day of December, even almost out   170
  of date!* Down on thy knees and make thee ready,
  sell some of thy clothes to buy thee a death's

---

145 *Cud* A deformation of the word God's in oaths and ex-
clamations (*Obs.* OED)
153 *corporal oath* an oath ratified by touching a sacred
object
158 *o'* ed. (a Q)
163 *botcher* bungler
167 *noses bored* Proverbial; To bore one's nose; to be
tricked or swindled (reference cited by *Tilley* N229)

head and put upon thy middle finger, your
least considering bawds do so much;* be not
thou worse, though thou art an old woman as   175
she is. I am cloyed with old stock fish,*
here's a young perch is sweeter meat by half.
Prithee, die before thy day if thou can'st,
that thou may'st not be counted a witch.

AGATHA   No, thou art a witch and I'll prove it.   180
I said I was with child, thou knew'st no other
but by sorcery. Thou said'st it was a cushion,
and so it is! [*Drops a pillow from under her
gown.*] Thou art a witch for it; I'll be sworn
to it!   185

GNOTHO   Ha, ha, ha, I told thee 'twas a cushion!
So get thy sheet ready, we'll see thee buried
as we go to church to be married.
Ex[*eunt* GNOTHO *and* SIREN]

AGATHA   Nay, I'll follow thee and show myself a
wife. I'll plague thee as long as I live with   190
thee, and I'll bury some money before I die that
my ghost may haunt thee afterward!* *Exit*

176 *old stock fish* technically, cod or other galoid fish
which has been split open for curing with salt but also used
in figurative expressions "as dead as a stock fish"
177 *perch* Pun; a fresh water fish common to the British
Isles;\ an elevated seat

Act IV, scene ii

Enter CLEANTHES

CLEANTHES
  What's that? Oh, nothing but the whispering wind
  Breathes through yon churlish hawthorn that grew rude
  As if it chid the gentle breath that kissed it.
  I cannot be too circumspect, too careful,
  For in these woods lies hid all my life's treasure,   5
  Which is too much ever to fear to lose,
  Though it be never lost. And if our watchfulness
  Ought to be wise and serious against a thief
  That comes to steal our goods, things all without us,
  That proves vexation often more than comfort,   10
  How mighty ought our providence to be
  To prevent those, if any such there were,
  That come to rob our bosom of our joys
  That only makes poor man delight to live!
  Pshaw! I'm too fearful. Fie, fie, who can hurt me?   15
  But 'tis a general cowardice that shakes
  The nerves of confidence. He that hides treasure
  Imagines everyone thinks of that place,
  When 'tis a thing least minded. Nay, let him change
  The place continually, where'er it keeps,   20
  There will the fear keep still. Yonder's the storehouse
  Of all my comfort now; and see, it sends forth
                              Enter HIPPOLITA
  A dear one to me. Precious chief of women,
  How does the good old soul? Has he fed well?

HIPPOLITA
  Beshrew me, sir, he made the heartiest meal today,   25
  Much good may it do his health!

CLEANTHES
  A blessing on thee, both for thy news and wish.

HIPPOLITA   His stomach, sir,

2 *churlish* ungracious
7-24 *Though it be . . . fed well?* ed. (Although Q gives
these lines to Hippolita, they are clearly a continuation of
Cleanthes' speech as Hippolita does not enter until ll. 21-
2.)
25 *Beshrew me*   '[I] thank you'

Is bettered wonderously since his concealment.

CLEANTHES
Heaven has a blessed work in it. Come, we're safe
                                        here,   30
I prithee, call him forth, the air's much wholesomer.

HIPPOLITA   Father! *Enter* LEONIDES

LEONIDES
How sweetly sounds the voice of a good woman!
It is so seldom heard, that when it speaks
It ravishes all senses. [*Turns to* CLEANTHES] Lists
                                    of honour!   35
I've a joy weeps to see you, 'tis so full,
So fairly fruitful.

CLEANTHES   [*Kneels*]
I hope to see you often and return
Loaden with blessings still to pour on some.
I find 'em all in my contented peace,   40
And lose not one in thousands. They're dispersed
So gloriously, I know not which are brightest!
I find 'em as angels are found, by legions:*
First in the love and honesty of a wife,
Which is the first and chiefest of all temporal
                                    blessings;   45
Next in yourself, which is the hope and joy
Of all my actions, my affairs, my wishes;
And, lastly, which crowns all, I find my soul
Crowned with the peace of 'em, the eternal riches,
Man's only portion for his heavenly marriage.   50

LEONIDES
Rise, thou art all obedience, love, and goodness.
I dare say that which thousand fathers cannot,
And that's my precious comfort, never son
Was in the way more of celestial rising!

33-5 *How sweetly . .... senses.* ed. (assigned to Hippolita
in Q)
35-7 *Lists of honour! . . . fruitful.* ed. (assigned to
Cleanthes in Q)
35 *Lists of honour!* an elliptical salutation meaning 'You
who are a rollcall of honourable acts' or, perhaps, 'You
whose name would appear in catalogues of honourable men'

Thou art so made of such ascending virtue   55
That all the powers of hell cannot sink thee. *A horn*
                              [*sounds off-stage*]

CLEANTHES   Ha!

LEONIDES   What was it disturbed my joy?

CLEANTHES   Did you not hear, as afar off?

LEONIDES   What, my excellent consort?   60

HIPPOLITA   I heard a –   *A horn* [*sounds again*]

CLEANTHES   Hark, again!

LEONIDES   Bless my joy, what ails it on a sudden?

CLEANTHES   Now, since lately.

LEONIDES   'Tis nothing but a symptom of thy care, man. 65

CLEANTHES   Alas, you do not hear well.

LEONIDES   What was it, daughter?

HIPPOLITA   I heard a sound twice.   *A horn* [*sounds a*
                                   third time]

CLEANTHES   Hark, louder and nearer.
  In, for the precious good of virtue, quick, sir!
               [HIPPOLITA *hurries* LEONIDES *away*]   70
  Louder and nearer yet, at hand, at hand!
  A hunting here 'tis strange, I never knew
  Game followed in these woods before. [*Re-enter*
                              HIPPOLITA]

HIPPOLITA   Now, let 'em come and spare not.
  Enter Duke [EVANDER], SIMONIDES, *Courtiers, and*
  [CRATILUS], *executioner.*

CLEANTHES
  Ha, is it not the duke? Look sparingly.   75

HIPPOLITA
  'Tis he, but what of that. Alas, take heed, sir,
  Your care will overthrow us.

CLEANTHES   Come, it shall not;
Let's set a pleasant face upon our fears
Though our hearts shake with horror. Ha, ha, ha!   80

EVANDER   Hark!

CLEANTHES   Prithee, proceed,
I'm taken with these light things infinitely
Since the old men's decease. Ha, so they parted,
ha, ha, ha!

EVANDER
Why, how should I believe this? Look, he's merry   85
As if he had no such charge. One with that care
Could never be so. Still, he holds his temper,
And 'tis the same, still with no difference,
He brought his father's corpse to the grave with.
He laughed thus then, you know.   90

1 COURTIER   Aye, he may laugh, my lord,
That shows but how he glories in his cunning,
And, perhaps, done more to advance his wit
Than to express affection to his father;
That only he has over-reached the law.   95

SIMONIDES
He tells you right, my lord, his own cousin-german
Revealed it first to me, a free-tongued woman,
And very excellent at telling secrets.

EVANDER   If a contempt can be so neatly carried,
It gives me cause of wonder.   100

SIMONIDES   Troth, my lord,
'Twill prove a delicate cozening, I believe.
I'd have no scrivener offer to come near it.

EVANDER   Cleanthes.

CLEANTHES   My loved lord?   105

EVANDER   [*Aside*]
Not moved a whit,

102 *cozening* trickery
103 *scrivener* copiest

Constant to lightness still. [*Turns back to Cleanthes*]
　　　　　　　　　　　　'Tis strange to meet you
Upon a ground so unfrequented, sir.
This does not sit your passion, you're for mirth
Or I mistake you much.　　　　　　　　　　110

CLEANTHES　　But, finding it
　Grow to a noted imperfection in me,
　For anything too much is vicious,
　I come to these disconsolate walks of purpose,
　Only to dull and take away the edge on it.　　115
　I ever had a greater zeal to sadness;
　A natural proportion, I confess, my lord,
　Before that cheerful accident fell out,
　If I may call a father's funeral cheerful
　Without wrong done to duty or my love.　　120

EVANDER
　It seems, then, you take pleasure in these walks, sir?

CLEANTHES　　Contemplative content, I do, my lord,
　They bring into my mind oft meditations
　So sweetly precious, that in the parting
　I find a shower of grace upon my cheeks,　　125
　They take their leave so feelingly.

EVANDER　　So, sir.

CLEANTHES　　Which is a kind of grave delight, my lord.

EVANDER
　And I've small cause, Cleanthes, to afford you
　The least delight that has a name.　　　　130

CLEANTHES　　My lord?

SIMONIDES　　[*Aside*]
　Now it begins to fadge.

1 COURTIER　　[*To* SIMONIDES]
　Peace! Thou art so greedy, Sim.

107 *lightness* ed. (lightning Q)
109 *sit* suit, appear fitting
132 *Now it begins to fadge.* 'Now the plan begins to suc-
ceed.'

EVANDER
  In your excess of joy, you have expressed
  Your rancour and contempt against my law.   135
  Your smiles deserve fining; you've professed
  Derision openly, even to my face,
  Which might be death, a little more incensed.
  You do not come for any freedom here,
  But for a project of your own.   140
  But, all that's known to be contentful to thee,
  Shall in the use prove deadly. Your life's mine
  If ever thy presumption do but lead thee
  Into these walks again, aye, or that woman.   [CLEANTHES
  and HIPPOLITA *draw back toward the woods.*] [*To courtiers*]
  I'll have 'em watched on purpose.   145

1 COURTIER   Now, now, his colour ebbs and flows!

SIMONIDES   Mark hers too.

HIPPOLITA
  Oh, who shall bring food to the poor old man now;
  Speak somewhat good, sir, or we're lost forever.

CLEANTHES
  Oh, you did wondrous ill to call me again;   150
  There are not words to help us. If I entreat
  'Tis found, that will betray us worse than silence.
  Prithee, let heaven alone and let's say nothing.

1 COURTIER   You've struck 'em dumb, my lord.

SIMONIDES   Look, how guilt looks!   155
  I would not have that fear upon my flesh
  To save ten fathers.

CLEANTHES   [*Still aside from the others*]
  He is safe still, is he not?

HIPPOLITA   Oh, you do ill to doubt it.

CLEANTHES   Thou art all goodness.   160

SIMONIDES   Now does your grace believe?

135 *rancour* animosity

EVANDER   'Tis too apparent.
  Search, make a speedy search, for the imposture
  Cannot be far off by the fear it sends.

CLEANTHES   Ha!   165

SIMONIDES
  [He] has the lapwing's cunning, I'm afraid, my lord,
  That cries most when she's farthest from the nest.*

CLEANTHES   Oh, we're betrayed!

HIPPOLITA   Betrayed, sir?

SIMONIDES   See, my lord,   170
  It comes out more and more still.   *Exeunt Courtiers*
                          and SIM[ONIDES]

CLEANTHES   Bloody thief!
  Come from that place, 'tis sacred homicide,
  'Tis not for thy adulterate hands to touch it!

HIPPOLITA   Oh miserable virtue,   175
  What distress art thou in at this minute?

CLEANTHES   Help me, thunder, for my power's lost!
  Angels, shoot plagues and help me!
  Why are these men in health and I so heart-sick?
  Or why should nature have that power in me   180
  To levy up a thousand bleeding sorrows,
  And not one comfort? Only makes me lie
  Like the poor mockery of an earthquake here,
  Panting with horror, and have not so much force
  In all my vengeance to shake a villain o' of me!   185
Enter Courtiers, SIMONIDES, [*and*] LEONIDES.

HIPPOLITA
  Use him gently and heaven will love you for it.

CLEANTHES   Father, oh father, now I see thee full
  In thy affection; thou 'rt a man of sorrow,
  But reverently becom'st it, that's my comfort.
  Extremity was never better graced   190

183 *Like the . . . eathquake* shaking
190 *extremity* adversity

Than with that look of thine. Oh, let me look still
For I shall lose it; all my joy and strength
Is e'en eclips'd together. [*Kneels before* EVANDER]
                              I transgressed
Your law, my lord, let me receive the sting on't
Be once just, sir, and let the offender die;   195
He's innocent in all, and I am guilty.

LEONIDES
  Your grace knows when affection only speaks,
  Truth is not always there. His love would draw
  An undeserved misery on his youth,
  And wrong a peace resolved, on both parts sinful. 200
  'Tis I am guilty of my own concealment
  And, like a worldly coward, injured heaven
  With fear to go to it. Now I see my fault
  And am prepared with joy to suffer for it.

EVANDER
  Go, given him quick dispatch, let him see death;   205
  And your presumption, sir, shall come to judgement.
                            [*Exit* EVANDER]
  Exeunt[SIMONIDES, *the* COURTIERS, *and* CRATILUS, *the*
  executioner] *with* LEONIDES.

HIPPOLITA He's going! Oh, he's gone, sir!

CLEANTHES   Let me rise.

HIPPOLITA   Why do you not then, and follow?

CLEANTHES   I strive for it.   210
  Is there no hand of pity that will ease me
  And take this villain from my heart awhile? [*Rises*]

HIPPOLITA   Alas, he's gone.

CLEANTHES   A worse supplies his place then,
  A weight more ponderous. I cannot follow.   215

HIPPOLITA   Oh, misery of afflication!

CLEANTHES   They will stay

Till I can come; they must be so good ever,
Though they be ne'er so cruel.
My last leave must be taken, think o' that,   220
And this last blessing given. I will not lose
That for a thousand consorts.

HIPPOLITA   That hope's wretched.

CLEANTHES   The unutterable stings of fortune!
All griefs are to be born, save this alone!   225
This, like a headlong torrent, overturns
The frame of nature;
For he that gives us life first, as a father,
Locks all his natural sufferings in our blood;
The sorrow that he feels, are our heads,   230
They are incorporate to us.

HIPPOLITA   Noble sir!

CLEANTHES   Let me behold thee well.

HIPPOLITA   Sir!

CLEANTHES   Thou should'st be good,   235
Or thou art a dangerous substance to be lodged
So near the heart of man.

HIPPOLITA   What means this, dear sir?

CLEANTHES
To thy trust only was this blessed secret
Kindly committed. 'Tis destroyed, thou see'st   240
What follows to be thought on it.

HIPPOLITA   Miserable!
Why, here's the unhappiness of woman still,
That having forfeited in old times their trust,
Now makes their faiths suspected that are just!
                          Enter EUGENIA   245

CLEANTHES   What shall I say to all my sorrows then,

222 *consorts* companions
229 *blood* ed. (blood to Q)
233 *thee* ed. (him Q)

That look for satisfaction?

EUGENIA   Ha, ha, ha, cousin!

CLEANTHES   How ill dost thou become this time!

EUGENIA   Ha, ha, ha,   250
Why, that's but your opinion, a young wench
Becomes the time at all times.
Now, coz, we're even! And you be remembered
You left a strumpet and a whore at home with me,
And such fine field-bed words which could not cost   255
                                                    you
Less than a father.

CLEANTHES   Is it come that way?

EUGENIA   Had you an uncle
He should go the same way too.

CLEANTHES   Oh, eternity!   260
What monster is this fiend in labour with?

EUGENIA
An ass-colt with two heads, that's she and you!
I will not lose so glorious a revenge
Not to be understood in it. I betray him,
And now we're even, you'd best keep it so.   265

CLEANTHES   Is there not poison yet enough to kill me?

HIPPOLITA   Oh, sir, forgive me, it was I betrayed him.

CLEANTHES   How!

HIPPOLITA   Aye.

CLEANTHES
The fellow of my heart 'twill speed me then.   270

255 *field-bed* a bed in an open field or upon the ground;
thus, vulgar, coarse (attrib. example cited in OED)
261 *in labour with* suffering to give birth to
262 *ass-colt* the young of an ass (numskull)
265 *it* ed. (you Q)

HIPPOLITA
    Her tears that never wept, and mine own pity
    Even cozened me together and stole from me
    This secret, which fierce death should not have
                                        purchased.

CLEANTHES
    Nay, then we're at an end, all we are false ones
    And ought to suffer: I was false to wisdom   275
    In trusting woman, thou wert false to faith
    In uttering of the secret, and thou false
    To goodness in deceiving such a pity.
    We are all tainted some way, but thou worst;
    And for thy infectious spots ought to die first.
                            [*Draws his sword*]   280

EUGENIA
    Pray turn your weapon, sir, upon your mistress;
    I come not so ill friended. Rescue, servants! [*Re*]*enter*
    SIMONIDES *and Courtiers* [*Swords drawn, they surround*
    EUGENIA]

CLEANTHES   Are you so whorishly provided?

SIMONIDES
    Yes, sir, she has more weapons at command than one.

EUGENIA   Put forward, man, thou art most sure to
                                        have me.   285

SIMONIDES [*Gets behind* EUGENIA]
    I shall be surer if I keep behind though.

EUGENIA   Now, servants, show your loves!

SIMONIDES   I'll show my love too, afar off.

EUGENIA   I love to be so courted! Woo me, there!

SIMONIDES
    I love to keep good weapons though ne'er fought;   290
    I'm sharper set within than I am without.

284 *weapons* Pun; swords, penises
291 *I'm sharper set . . . without.* Simonides means he is

HIPPOLITA   Oh, gentlemen! Cleanthes!

EUGENIA   Fight! Upon him!

HIPPOLITA
Thy thirst of blood proclaims thee now a strumpet.

EUGENIA   'Tis dainty, next to procreation fitting,   295
I'd either be destroying men or getting. *Enter*
Officers

1 OFFICER   Forbear, on your allegiance, gentlemen!
He's the duke's prisoner, and we seize upon him
To answer this contempt against the law.

CLEANTHES   I obey fate in all things.   300

HIPPOLITA   Happy rescue!

SIMONIDES
I would you'd seized upon him a minute sooner, it had
saved me a cut finger. I wonder how I came by it for
I never put my hand forth I'm sure. I think my own
sword did cut it, if truth were known; maybe the wire 305
in the handle. I have lived these five-and-twenty
years and never knew what colour my blood was before.
I never durst eat oysters, nor cut peck-loaves.

EUGENIA   You have shown your spirits, gentlemen, [*turns*
to SIMONIDES] but you have cut your finger.   310

SIMONIDES   Aye, the wedding finger too. A pox on it!

1 COURTIER   You'll prove a bawdy bachelor, Sim, to
have a cut upon your finger before you are married.*

more adept at the sexual act than one of self-defence
294 *blood* the supposed seat of animal or sensual appetite;
hence, the fleshy nature of man
294 *strumpet* a loose woman, a whore
296 *destroying* Pun; ruining the lives of; rendering
exhausted by copulation
296 *getting* Pun; acquiring; conceiving
308 *peck-loaves* loaves of bread made with a peck of
flour
311 *wedding finger* ring finger

SIMONIDES
  I'll never draw sword again to have such a jest put
                        upon me. [*Exeunt omnes*]

Act V, scene i

Sword and Mace carried before them, enter SIMONIDES
and the Courtiers.

SIMONIDES   Be ready with your prisoner,
  We'll sit instantly and rise before eleven,
  Or when we please. Shall we not follow, judges?

1 COURTIER   'Tis committed
  All to our power, censure, and pleasure, now   5
  The duke hath made us chief lords of this session;
  And we may speak by fits, or sleep by turns.

SIMONIDES   Leave that to us, but, whatsoe'er we do,
  The prisoner shall be sure to be condemned.
  Sleeping or waking, are we resolved on that   10
  Before we set upon him?

2 COURTIER   Make you question
  If not? Cleanthes? And our enemy!
  Nay, a concealer of his father too,
  A vile example in these days of youth.   15

SIMONIDES   If they were given to follow such examples,
  But sure I think they are not; howsoe'er,
  'Twas wickedly attempted, that's my judgment
  And it shall pass while I am in power to sit.
  Never by prince were such young judges made;   20
  But now the cause requires it, if you mark it.
  He must make young or none, for all the old ones,
  Their fathers, he hath sent a-fishing, and my
                          father's one.
  I humbly thank his highness.   *Enter* EUGENIA

1 COURTIER   Widow!   25

EUGENIA   You almost hit my name no[w] gentlemen;
  You come so wonderous near it, I admire you
  For your judgment.

10 *are we* ed. (we are Q)
13 *our* ed. (one Q)
23 *Their* ed. (We Q)
25 *Widow!* ed. (Widdows? Q)

SIMONIDES　　My wife that must be! She!

EUGENIA　　My husband goes upon his last hour now.　　　30

1 COURTIER　　On his last legs, I'm sure.

EUGENIA　　September the seventeenth,
I will not bate an hour on it; and tomorrow
His latest hour's expired.

2 COURTIER　　Bring him to judgment;　　　35
The jury's panelled and the verdict given
Ere he appears, we have ta'en course for that.

SIMONIDES　　And officers to attach the gray young man,
The youth of fourscore. Be of comfort, lady;
We shall no longer bosom January,　　　40
For that I will take order and provide
For you a lusty April.

EUGENIA　　The month that ought, indeed,
To go before May.

1 COURTIER　　Do as we have said;　　　45
Take a strong guard and bring him into court.
Lady Eugenia, see this charge performed
That, having his life forfeited by the law,
He may relieve his soul.

EUGENIA　　Willingly!　　　50
From shaven chins never came better justice
Than these new-touched by reason.

SIMONIDES　　What you do, do suddenly we charge you,
For we purpose to make but a short sessions.
Ah, new business!　　　55
Enter HIPPOLITA

31 *On his last legs* Proverbial; To be (to go) on one's
last legs (first reference in *Tilley* L193).
36 *panelled* trans. empanelled; constituted (ref. in OED)
37 *Ere* ed. (Ever Q)
38 *attach* arrest
40 *January* old age
42 *April* an April gentleman; a man newly-married (Partridge)
44 *May* May-games; frolics; here, sexual games

1 COURTIER
The fair Hippolita, now, what's your suit?

HIPPOLITA   Alas, I know not how to style you yet;
To call you judges doth not suit your years,
For heads and beards show more antiquity.
Yet sway yourselves with equity and truth   60
And I'll proclaim you reverend and repeat,
"Once in my lifetime I have seen grave heads
Placed upon young men's shoulders."

2 COURTIER   Hark, she flouts us,
And, thinks to make us monstrous.   65

HIPPOLITA   Prove not so,
For yet, methinks, you bear the shapes of men,
Though nothing more than mercy beautifies
To make you appear angels. But, if [you] crimson
Your name and power with blood and cruelty,   70
Suppress fair virtue and enlarge of old vice,
Both against heaven and nature draw your sword,
Make either will or humour turn the soul
Of your created greatness, and in that
Oppose all goodness, I must tell you there   75
You're more than monstrous. In the very act,
You change yourself to devils.

1 COURTIER   She's a witch!
Hark, she begins to conjure!

SIMONIDES   Time, you see, is short,   80
Much business' now on foot. Shall I
Give her her answer?

2 COURTIER   None upon the bench
More learnedly can do it.

SIMONIDES   Hem, hem, hem, then list'.   85
I wonder at thine impudence, young huswife,

59 *For* ed. (Nor Q)   59 *beards* Gifford (brains Q)
60 *equity* fairness
68 *mercy beautifies* Bullen (meerly beautifeans Q)
69 *crimson* sully, disgrace   85 *list'* listen
86 *huswife* mistress; or, perhaps something like 'you saucy
one'

That thou dar'st plead for such a base offender.
Conceal a father past his time to die!
What son and heir would have done this but he?

1 COURTIER   I vow, not I.   90

HIPPOLITA   Because we are parricides!
  And how can comfort be derived from such
  That pity not their fathers.

2 COURTIER
  You are fresh and fair, practise young women's ends;
  When husbands are distressed, provide them friends.   95

SIMONIDES
  I'll set him forward for thee without fee,
  Some wives would pay for such a courtesy

HIPPOLITA
  Times of amazement, where doth goodness dwell!
  I sought for charity, but knock at hell!   *Exit*
                                    [HIPPOLITA]
  Enter EUGENIA, *with* LISANDER *prisoner,* [*and*] *a guard.*

SIMONIDES   Eugenia, come! Command a second guard   100
  To bring Cleanthes in. We'll not sit long,
  My stomach strives to dinner.

EUGENIA   Now, servants, may a lady be so bold
  To call your power so low?

SIMONIDES   A mistress may;   105
  She can make all things low, then in that language
  There can be no offence.

EUGENIA   The time's now come
  Of manumissions, take him into bonds,

91 *parricides* father-murderers
95 *friends* kisses (as in the Proverb 'kiss and make up');
or, perhaps, bed-companions
96 *I'll set him . . . without fee* Bullen (I'le set him forward fee thee; without fee, in italics, appears as if s.d. Q)
98 *where doth* ed. (what duty Q)
102 *strives* struggles toward
109 *manumissions*   formal releases from slavery

And I am then at freedom.

2 COURTIER   This the man!
He hath left of late to feed on snakes,
His beard's turned white again.*

1 COURTIER
Is it possible these gouty legs danced lately,
And shattered in a galliard?   115

EUGENIA   Jealousy
And fear of death can work strange prodigies.

2 COURTIER   The nimble fencer this, that made me tear
And traverse 'bout the chamber?

SIMONIDES   Aye, and gave me   120
Those elbow healths, the hangman take him for it!
They had almost fetched my heart on it.   The Dutch
                                              vennie
I swallowed pretty well, but the half pike
Had almost pepper'd me.   But had I took,
Being swollen, I had cast my lungs out.   125
A flourish, Enter the Duke [EVANDER, *and* CRATILUS,
                           the executioner.]

2 COURTIER   Peace!   The duke!

EVANDER   Nay, take your seats.   Who's that?

SIMONIDES   May it please your highness,
'Tis old Lisander.

EVANDER   And brought in by his wife!   A worthy precedent
Of one that no way would offend the law,

115 *shattered*   were thrown about
117 *prodigies*   wonders
121 *elbow healths*   toasts
122 *fetched my heart*   'made me vomit my heart out'
124 *pepper'd* Bullen   (prepared Q)
s.d. *A flourish* ed.   (A flemish Q; given as a line spoken
by Evander)
127 *take* ed.   (bathe Q)
126-7 *Peace . . . . Who's that?*   (In the Q both these lines
are given to the second Courtier)

And should not pass away without remark.
[*Turns to* LISANDER] You had been looked for long.

LISANDER   But never fit
  To die till now, my lord, my sins and I   135
  Have been but newly parted. Much ado
  I had to get them leave me, or be taught
  That difficult lesson, how to learn to die.
  I never thought there had been such an act,
  And 'tis the only discipline we are born for.   140
  All studies as are, are but as circular lines
  And death the centre where they must all meet.
  I now can look upon thee, erring woman,
  And not be vexed with jealousy; on young men,
  And no way envy their delicious health,   145
  Pleasure and strength, all which were once mine own,
  And mine must be their's one day.

EVANDER   You have tamed him.

SIMONIDES   And know how to dispose him. That,
                          my liege,
  Hath been before determined. [*Turns to* LISANDER] You
                               confess 150
  Yourself of full age?

LISANDER   Yes, and prepared to inherit –

EUGENIA   Your place above!

SIMONIDES   Of which the hangman's strength
  Shall put him in possession.   155

LISANDER   'Tis still
  To take me willing and in mind to die,
  And such are, when the earth grows weary of them,
  Most fit for heaven.

SIMONIDES   The court shall make his mittimus   160
  And send him thither presently.

153-63 *Your place above* . . . . *In the meantime* ed. (These
lines are another very confused passage in the Q text.
Emendations are taken in part from Gifford and Bullen but
greater care has been taken to retain as much of the
original as possible.)
160 *mittimus* warrant of custody

EVANDER   Guard! Away to death with him! [*Exit* CRATILUS
                                          with LISANDER]

SIMONIDES   In the meantime -
    Enter a guard with CLEANTHES, HIPPOLITA *weeping after him.*
    So! See, another person brought to the bar!

1 COURTIER   The arch malefactor!   165

2 COURTIER   The grand offender! The most refractory
    To all good order! 'Tis Cleanthes, he -

SIMONIDES
    That would have sons grave fathers ere their fathers
    Be sent unto their graves.

EVANDER   There will be expectation   170
    In your severe proceedings against him,
    His act being so capital?

SIMONIDES   Fearful and bloody!
    Therefore we charge these women leave the court
    Lest they should swoon to hear it..   175

EUGENIA   Aye, in expectation
    Of a most happy freedom! *Exit* [EUGENIA]

HIPPOLITA   Aye, with the apprehension
    Of a most sad and desolate widowhood! *Exit* [HIPPOLITA]

1 COURTIER   We bring him to the bar.   180

2 COURTIER   Hold up your hand, sir.

CLEANTHES
    More reverence to the place than to the persons!
    To the one I offer up a [spreading] palm [*Lifts arm*
                          with hand outstretched]
    Of duty and obedience showed [th]us to heaven,
    Imploring justice which was never wanting   185
    Upon that bench whilst their own fathers sat.
    But unto you, my hand's contracted, thus! [*Clenches*
                          fist, threateningly]

166 *offender* ed. (offenders Q)   167 *order* ed. (orders Q)
172 *capital* serious; concerning a life and death matter
175 *swoon* ed. (stand Q)

As threatening vengeance against murderers;
For they that kill in thought, shed innocent blood!
With pardon to your highness, too much passion   190
Made me forget your presence and the place;
I now am called too.

EVANDER   All our majesty
And power we have to pardon or condemn,
Is now conferred on them.   195

SIMONIDES   And these we'll use
Little to thine advantage.

CLEANTHES   I expect it.
And as to these, I look no mercy from [them]
And much less mean to entreat it. I thus now   200
Submit me [to] the emblems of your power, I mean
The sword and bench. But, my most reverend judges,
E'er you proceed to sentence, for I know
You have given me lost, will you resolve me one thing?

1 COURTIER   So it be briefly questioned.   205

2 COURTIER   Show your honour,
Day spends itself apace.

CLEANTHES   My lords, it shall
Resolve me then. Where are your filial tears,
Your mourning habits, and sad hearts become,   210
That should attend your fathers' funeral?
Though the strict law, which I will not accuse
Because a subject, snatched away their lives,
It doth not bar you to lament their deaths;
Or, if you cannot spare one sad suspire,   215
It doth not bid you laugh them to their graves,
Lay subtle trains to antedate their years,
To be the sooner seized of their estates.
Oh time of age! Where's that Aeneas now,
Who, letting all his jewels to the flames,   220
Forgetting country, kindred, treasure, friends,
Fortunes, and all things save the name of son,
Which you so much forget? Go like Aeneas,

193 *our* ed. (one Q)
200 *mean* ed. (showne Q)
214 *you* ed. (them Q)

Who took his bedrid father on his back,
And with the sacred load, to him no burden,   225
Hewed out his way through blood, through fire, through
Even all the armed streets of bright-burning Troy,
Only to save a father.*

SIMONIDES   We have no leisure now
To hear lessons read from Virgil, we are past   230
                                          school
And all this time thy judges.

2 COURTIER   'Tis fit
That we proceed to sentence.

1 COURTIER   You are the mouth,
And now 'tis fit to open.   235

SIMONIDES   Justice, indeed,
Should ever be close-eared and open-mouthed,
That is, to hear little and speak much.
Lo, then, Cleanthes, there's none can be
A good son and a bad subject, for if princes,   240
Becalled the people's fathers, then the subjects
Are all his sons, and he that flouts the prince
Doth disobey his father. There ye are gone.

1 COURTIER   And not to be recovered.

SIMONIDES   And again –   245

2 COURTIER   If he be gone once, call him not again.

SIMONDIES   I say again, this act of thine expresses
A double disobedience. As our princes
Are fathers, so they are our sovereigns too,
And he that doth rebel against sovereignty   250
Doth commit treason in the height of degree.
And now, thou art quite gone.

1 COURTIER   Our brother in commission

236-7 *Justice, indeed . . . speak much.* a comic reversal of
the Proverb; It is better to play with the ears than the
tongue (see *Tilley* E 17)
238 *hear* ed. (hear him Q)
253 *in commission* with endowed authority

Hath spoke his mind both learnedly and neatly,
And I can add but little, howsoever   255
It shall send him packing.
He that begins a fault that wants example,
Ought to be made example for the fault.

CLEANTHES   A fault! No longer can I hold myself
   To hear vice upheld and virtue thrown down.   260
   A fault! Judge, then, I desire, where it lieth,
   In those that are my judges or in me.
   Heaven stand on my side! Pity love and duty!

SIMONIDES
   Where are they, sir? Who sees them but yourself?

CLEANTHES   Not you, and I am sure;   265
   You never had the gracious eyes to see them.
   You think you arraign me, but I hope
   To sentence you at the bar.

2 COURTIER   [*Laughing*]
   That would show brave!

CLEANTHES   This were the judgment seat. We [k]now   270
   The heaviest crimes that ever made up
   Unnaturalness in humanity,
   You are found foul . and guilty by the jury
   Made of your fathers' curses which have brought
   Vengeance impending on you, and I now   275
   Am forced to pronounce judgment of my judges.
   The common laws of reason and of nature
   Condemn you *ipso facto!* You are parricides,
   And if you marry will beget the like,
   Who, when grown to full maturity,   280
   Will hurry you, their fathers, to your graves.
   Like traitors, you take counsel from the living;
   Of upright judgment, you would rob the bench;

267 *arraign* charge
268 *bar* the final judgment
269 *brave* bravado
275 *impending* overhanging
278 *ipso facto* by the fact itself
279 *like* ed. (1yar Q)
280 *when grown* ed. (when y'are grown Q)
281 *your* ed. (their Q)

Experience and discretion snatch away
From the earth's face; turn all into disorder,   285
Imprison virtue, and enfranchise vice;
And put the sword of justice into the hands of
Boys and madmen.

SIMONIDES   Well, well, have you done, sir?

CLEANTHES   I have spoke my thoughts.   290

SIMONIDES   Then I'll begin and end.

EVANDER   [*Steps forward*]
'Tis time I now begin,
Where your commission ends.
Cleanthes, you come from the bar.
Because I know you're severally disposed,   295
I here invite you to an object will, no doubt,
Work in you contrary effects.
Music!
Music sounds. [LISANDER, LEONIDES, CREON,] *and the
                              old men appear.*

CLEANTHES
Pray heaven I dream not! Sure he moves, talks
                              comfortably
As joy can wish a man. If he be changed   300
Far above from me, he is not ill-treated.
His face doth promise fullness of content
And glory hath a part in it.

LEONIDES   Oh, my son!

EVANDER
You that can claim acquaintance with these lads,   305
Talk freely.

SIMONIDES   I can see none there that's worth
One hand to you from me.

284 *snatch* ed. (snatcht Q)
286 *enfranchise* give freedom to
295 *severally disposed* inclined to judge matters on individual merit
s.d. *Music sounds* ed. (Musick, Sons Q)
301 *ill-treated* ed. (ill intreated Q)

EVANDER   [*To* CLEANTHES]
   These are thy judges, and by their grave law
   I find thee clear but these delinquents guilty.   310
   You must change places, for 'tis so decreed
   Such just pre-eminence hath thy goodness gained,
   Thou art the judge now, they the men arraigned.

1 COURTIER   Here's fine dancing, gentlemen!

2 COURTIER   Is thy father amongst them?   315

SIMONIDES
   Oh, a pox! I saw him the first thing I looked on
   Alive again! 'Slight, I believe now a father
   Hath as many lives as a mother.

CLEANTHES   'Tis full as blessed as 'tis wonderful!
   Oh, bring me back to the same law again,   320
   I'm fouler than all these! Seize on me, officers,
   And bring me to new sentence.

EVANDER   What's all this?

CLEANTHES   A fault not to be pardoned!
   Unnaturalness is but sun's shadow to it.   325

SIMONIDES
   I am glad of that, I hope the case may alter
   And I turn judge again.

EVANDER   [*To* CLEANTHES]
   Name your offence.

CLEANTHES   That I should be so vile
   As once to think you cruel.   330

EVANDER   Is that all?

---

314 *Here's fine dancing* 'This presents a quandary;' or, if
dancing refers to being hanged, 'Here's evidence for our
execution.'
316-8 *Oh, a pox! . . . mother.* ed. (lines given to Cleanthes
in Q)
319-22 *'Tis full . . . new sentence.* ed. (lines given to
Simonides in Q)
323 *What's all this?* ed. (lines given to Cleanthes in Q)

'Twas pardoned e'er confessed. [*To old men*] You
that have sons,
If they be worthy, here may challenge them.

CREON
I should have one amongst them, had he had grace
To have retained that name.   335

SIMONIDES   [*Kneels*]
I pray you, father.

CREON   That name I know
Hath been long since forgot.

SIMONIDES   [*Aside*]
I find but small comfort in remembering it now.

EVANDER
Cleanthes, take your place with these grave fathers   340
And read what in that table is inscribed. [*Hands him
a paper*]
Now set these at the bar,
And read, Cleanthes, to the dread and terror
Of disobedience and unnatural blood.

CLEANTHES   [*Reads*]
It is decreed by the grave and learned council of   345
Epire, that no son and heir shall be held capable of
his inheritance at the age of one-and-twenty, unless
he be at that time as mature in obedience, manners,
and goodness.

SIMONIDES   Sure, I shall never be at full age then,   350
though I live to an hundred years, and that's nearer
by twenty than the last statute allowed.

1 COURTIER   A terrible act!

CLEANTHES   *Moreover is enacted, that all sons aforesaid,*
whom either this law, or their own grace, whom it   355
shall reduce into the true method of duty, virtue, and

333 *may* ed. (my Q)
333 *challenge* confront
340 *place* ed. (places Q) 341 *table*   tablet upon which
laws were written   348 *mature* ed. (nature Q)

affection, and relate their trial and approbation
from Cleanthes, the son of Leonides, -
From me, my lord?

EVANDER
From none but you as fullest. Proceed, sir.   360

CLEANTHES   *Whom for his manifest virtues, we make such*
judge and censure of youth, and the absolute reference
of life and manners.

SIMONIDES   This is a brave world! When a man should
be selling land, he must be learning manners. Is it 365
not, my masters? *Enter EUGENIA*

EUGENIA   What's here do to? My suitors at the bar?
The old band shines again, oh miserable! *She swoons*

EVANDER   Read the law over to her, 'twill awake her.
'Tis one deserves small pity.   370

CLEANTHES   [*Reads again*]
Lastly, it is ordained that all such wives now
whatsoever that shall design the[*ir*] *husbands' death*
to be soon rid of them and entertain suitors in their
husbands' lifetime, -

SIMONIDES   You had best read that a little louder,   375
For if anything that will bring her to herself again,
And find her tongue.

CLEANTHES   *Shall not presume, on the penalty of our*
heavy displeasure, to marry within ten years after.

EUGENIA
That law's too long by nine years and a half;   380
I'll take my death upon it, so shall most women.

354-8 *Moreover . . . Leonides* ed. (lines given in Q as a
continuation of first Courtier's speech)
357 *approbation* attestation
360 *fullest* most able
361 *manifest* obvious
362 *censure* corrector
368 *band* ed. (baud Q)

CLEANTHES
And those incontinent women so offending, to be judge[d]
and censured by Hippolita, wife to Cleanthes.

EUGENIA
Of all the rest, I'll not be judge[d] by her. *Enter*
                                              HIPPOLITA

CLEANTHES   Ah, here she comes. Let me prevent thy   385
                                              joys,
    Prevent them but in part and hide the rest,
    Thou hast not strength enough to bear them else.

HIPPOLITA   Leonides! *She faints*

CLEANTHES   I feared it all this while.
    I knew 'twas past thy power, Hippolita.   390
    What contrariety is in women's blood?
    One faints for spleen and anger, she for grace.

EVANDER
    Of sons and wives, we see the worst and best;
    May future ages yield Hippolitas
    Many, but few like thee, Eugenia.   400
    Let no Simonides' henceforth have a fame,
    But all blest sons live in Cleanthes name.
    Music [sounds from off-stage]
    Ha, what strange kind of melody was that?
    Yet give it entrance, whatsoe'er it be.
    This day is all devout to liberty.   405
    Enter Clown [GNOTHO] and Wench [SIREN], the rest
    with the old women, [AGATHA] the Clown's wife;
    *music, and a bride's cake to the wedding.**

GNOTHO   Fiddlers crowd on, crowd on, let no man lay a
    block in your way. Crowd on, I say!

EVANDER
    Stay the crowd awhile, let's know the reason of this
                                              jollity.

CLEANTHES   Sirrah, do you know where you are?

382 *incontinent* unchaste
392 *spleen* temper
405 *devout* devoted   s.d. *bride's cake* ed. (bridecake Q)

GNOTHO
      Yes, sir, I am here, now here, and now here again,
                                                    sir.   410

LISANDER   Your hat's too high-crowned, the duke in
                                            presence.

GNOTHO   The duke? As he is my sovereign, I do give
      him two crowns for it, and that's equal change all
      the world over. As I am lord of the day, being my
      marriage day the second, I do advance bonnet. Crowd 415
      on afore!

LEONIDES   Good sir, a few words if you'll vouchsafe
                                                  'em,
      Or will you be forced?

GNOTHO   Forced? I would the duke himself would say so!

EVANDER
      I think he dares, sir, and does. If you stay not   420
      You shall be forced.

GNOTHO   I think so, my lord, and good reason too.
      Shall not I stay when your grace says I shall? I
      were unworthy to be a bridegroom in any part of
      your highness' dominions then. Will it please you   425
      to taste of the wedlock courtesy?*

EVANDER   Oh, by no means, sir. You shall not deface
      So fair an ornament for me.

GNOTHO
      If your grace be pleased to be cakated, say so.

---

411 *too high-crowned* too tall in the head-piece; too highly
ornamented; or, as the crown also means the top part of the
skull, Lisander may be pointing out that Gnotho should have
his hat off in the duke's presence. 412 *sovereign* supreme
ruler; a gold coin worth, at this time, about 10s
413 *crowns* gold coins worth 5s   415 *advance* raise
415-16 *crowd on* hasten on; continue fiddling
426 *taste of the wedlock courtesy* pun; to have a piece of
the wedding cake; to copulate with the bride (see notes)
429 *cakated* humorous nonce-formation intended to mean 'to
serve with cake' (OED); also a bawdy pun on 'to cake' [cack]

EVANDER   And which might be your fair bride, sir?   430

GNOTHO   This is my two-for-one that must be *uxor uxoris*,
The remedy *doloris*,* and the very *syceum amoris*.

EVANDER   And hast thou any else?

GNOTHO   I have an older, my lord, for other uses.

CLEANTHES   My lord, I do observe a strange decorum
                                        here.   435
These that do lead this day of jollity,
Do march with music and most mirthful cheeks;
Those that do follow, sad and woefully,
Nearer the 'haviour of a funeral
Than a wedding.   440

EVANDER   Tis true, pray expound that, sir.

GNOTHO   As the destiny of the day falls out, my lord,
one goes out to wedding, another goes to hanging.
And your grace, in the due consideration, shalt find
'em much alike; the one hath the ring upon her   445
finger, the other a halter about her neck. "I take
thee Beatrice," says the bridegroom. "I take thee
Agatha," says the hangman; and both say together,
"to have and to hold 'til death do part us."

EVANDER
This is not yet plain enough to my understanding.   450

GNOTHO   If further your grace examine it, you shall
find I show myself a dutiful subject and obedient to
the law. [Of] myself, these my good friends and
your good subjects, [and] our old wives whose days
are ripe and their lives forfeit to the law, only   455
myself, more forward than the rest, am already
provided of my second choice.

meaning 'to void excrement' and on 'to be cocky' meaning 'to
be lecherous.'
431 *uxor uxoris* best of all possible wives
432 *remedy doloris* cure for sadness (see notes)
432 *syceum amoris* provider of love (*syceum*: the female
pudend)
453 *these* ed. (with these Q)

EVANDER   Oh, take heed, sir, you'll run yourself into
                                                    danger
   If the law finds you with two wives at once.
   There's a shrewd premunire.   460

GNOTHO   I have taken leave of the old, my lord; I
   have nothing to say to her, she's going to sea. Your
   grace knows whither better than I do. She has a strong
   wind with her, it stands full in her poop. When you
   please, let her disembogue.   465

COOK   And the rest of her neighbours with her whom
   we present to the satisfaction of your highness' law.

GNOTHO   And so we take our leaves and leave them to
   your highness. Crowd on!

EVANDER   Stay, stay, you are too forward. Will you
                                              marry   470
   And your wife yet living?

GNOTHO   Alas, she'll be dead before we can get to
   church, if your grace would set her in the way. I
   would dispatch her, I have a venture on it which
   would return me, if your highness would make a   475
   little more haste, two for one.

EVANDER
   Come, my lords, we must sit again. Here's a case
   Craves a most serious censure.

COOK   Now they shall be dispatched out of the way.

GNOTHO
   I would they were gone [at] once. The time goes away. 480

460 *shrewd* ill-disposed
460 *premunire* predicament
462 *going to sea* Proverbial; The sea and the gallows
refuse none; The sea refuses no river (see *Tilley* S178; 181)
464 *wind* Pun; breeze, smell
464 *poop* Pun; the stern of a ship; the hinder parts of a
man or animal, the posteriors, rump *(colloq.* or *vulgar. Obs.*
OED)
465 *disembogue* ed. (disemboge Q) to sail forth as from a
river into the open sea

EVANDER   Which is the wife unto the forward bridegroom?

AGATHA   I am, and it please your grace.

EVANDER   Trust me, a lusty woman, able-bodied,
And well-blooded cheeks.

GNOTHO   Oh, she paints, my lord. She was a chamber-   485
maid once and learned it of her lady.

EVANDER   Sure, I think she cannot be so old.

AGATHA
Truly, I think so too, and please your grace.

GNOTHO   Two to one with your grace of that, she's
threescore by the book.   490

LEONIDES   Peace, sirrah, you're too loud!

COOK   Take heed, Gnotho, if you move the duke's
patience, 'tis an edge tool. But a work and a
blow, he cuts off your head.

GNOTHO   Cut off my head? Away, ignorant! He knows   495
it costs more in the hair; he does not use to cut
off many such heads as mine. I will talk to him
too. If he cut off my head, I'll give him my ears.
I say my wife is at full age for the law. The
clerk shall take his oath and the church book shall   500
be sworn too.

EVANDER   My lords, I leave this censure to you.

LEONIDES   Then, first, this fellow does deserve
                              punishment
For offering up a lusty able woman
Which may do service to the commonwealth,   505
Where the law craves one impotent and useless.

485 *paints* uses cosmetics
496 *it costs more in the hair* it goes against nature(?)
(see *Tilley* H18)
496 *use* make it a habit

CREON   Therefore, to be severely punished
  For thus attempting a second marriage
  His wife yet living.

LISANDER Nay, to have it trebled,   510
  That even the day and instant when he should mourn
  As a kind husband to her funeral,
  He leads a triumph to the scorn of it,
  Which unseasonable joy ought to be punished
  With all severity.   515

BUTLER
  The fiddles will be in a foul case too, by and by.

LEONIDES   Nay, further, it seems he has a venture
  Of two for one at his second marriage,
  Which cannot be but a conspiracy
  Against the former.   520

GNOTHO   A mess of wise old men!

LISANDER   Sirrah, what can you answer to all these?

GNOTHO   Ye are good old men and talk as age will give
  you leave. I would speak with the youthful duke
  himself; he and I may speak of things that shall be 525
  thirty or forty years after you are dead and rotten.
  Alas, you are here to-day and gone to sea tomorrow.

EVANDER
  In truth, sir, then I must be plain with you.
  The law that should take away your old wife from you,
  The which I do perceive was your desire,   530
  Is void and frustrate, so for the rest.
  There has been since another parliament
  Has cut it off.

GNOTHO   I see your grace is disposed to be pleasant.

EVANDER   Yes, you might perceive that, I had not   535
  Else thus dallied with your follies.

516 *The fiddles . . . foul case* Pun; The musicians will
put away their instruments; the cheaters will be in an
unpleasant law-suit.

GNOTHO   I'll talk further with your grace when I come
   back from church. In the meantime, you know what to
   do with the old women.

EVANDER   Stay, sir, unless in the meantime you mean   540
   I cause a gibbet to be set up in your way,
   And hang you at your return.

AGATHA   Oh, gracious prince!

EVANDER   Your old wives cannot die to-day by any
   Law of mine. For aught I can say to 'em   545
   They may, by a new edict, bury you,
   And then, perhaps, you pay a new fine too.

GNOTHO   This is fine, indeed!

AGATHA
   Oh, gracious prince, may he live a hundred years more.

COOK
   Your venture is not like to come in to-day, Gnotho.   550

GNOTHO   Give me the principal back.

COOK   Nay, by my troth, we'll venture still, and I'm
   sure we have as ill a venture of it as you for we
   have taken old wives of purpose, where that we had
   thought to have put away at this market and now we   555
   cannot utter a pennyworth.

EVANDER   Well, sirrah, you were best to discharge
   Your new charge, and take your old one to you.

GNOTHO
   Oh music! No music, but prove most doleful trumpets;
   Oh bride! No bride, but thou mayest prove a
                                            strumpet;   560
   Oh venture! No venture, I have for one now none;
   Oh wife! Thy life is sav'd when I hoped it had been
                                                gone.
   Case up your fruitless strings! No penny, no wedding;

541 *gibbet* gallows
550 *Gnotho* ed. (Gnothoes Q)
551 *principal* original investment

Case up thy maidenhead! No priest, no bedding.*
Avaunt my venture, it can ne'er be restored,   565
'Til Ag, my old wife, be thrown overboard.
Then, come again, old Ag, since it must be so,
Let bride and venture with woeful music go.

COOK   What for the bride's cake, Gnotho?

GNOTHO   Let it be mouldy, now 'tis out of season;   570
  Let it grow out of date, current and reason;
  Let it be chipped and chopped, and given to chickens,
  No more is got by that than William Dickens
  Got by his wooden dishes!*
  Put up your plums as fiddlers put up pipes,   575
  The wedding dashed, the bridegroom
  Weeps and wipes!
  Fiddlers farewell, and now, without perhaps,
  Put up your fiddles as you put up scraps.

LISANDER   This passion has given some satisfaction
                                              yet,   580
  My lord, I think you'll pardon him now,
  With all the rest, so they live honestly
  With the wives they have.

EVANDER   Oh, most freely! Free pardon to all!

COOK   Aye, we have deserved our pardons if we can   585
  live honestly with such reverend wives that have
  no motion in 'em but their tongues.

AGATHA   Heaven bless your grace, you're a just prince.

GNOTHO   All hopes dashed; the clerk's duties lost;
  Venture gone; my second wife divorced;   590
  And, which is worse, the old one come back again!
  Such voyages are made now-a-days.
  I will weep two salt of my nose, besides these two

569 *bride's cake* ed. (bridecake Q)   571 *reason* pronounced
raisin; thus date, currant, & raisin   575 *plums* dried
grapes or raisins   579 *scraps* the left-overs of a meal
(musicians were fed after the banquet was over)
586 *reverend* worthy   593 *my* ed. (our Q)
592-4 *Such voyages . . . of fresh water.* 'In these days of
such reversals one may expect the same fountain to yield

fountains of fresh water. Your grace had been more
kind to your young subjects. Heaven bless and mend   595
your laws that they do not gull your poor country
men [in this] fashion. But I am not the first by
forty that has been undone by the law; 'tis but a
folly to stand upon terms. I take my leave of your
grace, as well as mine eyes will give me leave. I   600
would they had been asleep in their beds when they
opened 'em to see this day! Come, Ag, come, Ag.
[*Exit* GNOTHO, AGATHA, *and the fiddlers*]

CREON   Were not you all my servants?

COOK   During your life, as we thought, sir, but our
young master turned us away.   605

CREON   [*To* SIMONIDES]
How headlong [a] villain wert thou in thy ruin!

SIMONIDES
I followed the fashion, sir, as other young men did.
If you were as we thought you had been,
We should ne'er have come for this, I warrant you.
We did not feed, after the old fashion, on beef   610
And mutton and such like.

CREON   [*Turning back to servants*]
Well, what damage or charge you have run
Yourselves into by marriage, I cannot help,
Nor deliver you from your wives, them you must keep.
Yourselves shall again retain me.   615

ALL   We thank your lordship for your love, and must
thank ourselves for our bad bargains. [*Exit the
servants and old wives*]

EVANDER   Cleanthes, you delay the power of law

salt and fresh water' (see *James* iii:12 Can the fig tree, my
brethren, bear olive berries? either a vine, figs? so can no
fountain yield salt water and fresh). There may also be
the extended implication that whereas Gnotho had expected
figs (Siren, his *syceum amoris*), he got the bitter olive
berry (Agatha).
608 *were* ed. (have Q)
615 *me* ed. (to me Q)

To be inflicted on these misgoverned men
That filial duty have so far transgressed.   620

CLEANTHES   My lord, I see a satisfaction
Meeting the sentence, even preventing it,
Beating my words back in their utterance.
See, sir, there's salt sorrow bringing forth fresh
And new duties, as the sea propagates. [SIMONIDES 625
and other Courtiers kneel]
The elephants have found their joints too.* Why,
Here's humility able to bind up
The punishing hands of the severest masters,
Much more the gentle fathers.

SIMONIDES   I had ne'er thought to have been brought 630
so low as my knees again, but, since there's no
remedy, - Fathers, reverend fathers, as you ever
hope to have good sons and heirs, a handful of pity!
We confess we have deserved more than we are willing
to receive at your hands, though sons can never   635
deserve too much of their fathers, as shall appear
afterwards.

CREON   And, what way can you decline your feeding now?
You cannot retire to beefs and muttons, sure.

SIMONIDES   Alas, sir, you see a good pattern for   640
that! Now we have laid by our high and lusty
meats and are down to our mary bones already.

CREON
Well, sir, rise to virtues! [*They rise*] We'll bind
you now;
You that were too weak yourselves to govern,
By others shall be governed.   645

LISANDER   Cleanthes,
I meet your justice with reconcilement.

624 *salt sorrow* tears
624-5 *See, sir . . . propagates.* Proverbial; the sea refuses no river (is never full) (see *Tilley* S181)
626 *The elephants have found their joints.* 'The penitent
sons are kneeling.' (see notes)
641 *mary bones* knees (prayer bones); marrow bones
643 *bind* ten thousand

If there be tears of faith in woman's breast,
I have received a myriad which confirms me
To find a happy renovation.   650

CLEANTHES   [*Turns to* LEONIDES]
Here's virtue's throne,
Which I'll embellish with my dearest jewels
Of love and faith, peace and affection!
This is the altar of my sacrifice,
Where daily my devoted knees shall bend.   655
Age-honoured shrine! Time still so love you
That I so long may have you in mine eye,
Until my memory lose your beginning.
For you, great prince, long may your fame survive,
Your justice and your wisdom never die!   660
Crown of your crown, the blessing of your land,
Which you reach to her from your regent's hand!

LEONIDES   Oh, Cleanthes, had you with us tasted
The entertainment of our retirement,
Feared and exclaimed on in your ignorance,   665
You might have sooner died upon the wonder
Than any rage or passion for our loss.
A place at hand we were all strangers in;
So sphered about with music, such delights,
Viands, and attendance, and, once a day   670
So cheered with a royal visitant,
That ofttimes waking, our unsteady phantasies
Would question whether we yet lived or no,
Or had possession of that paradise
Where angels be the guard.   675

EVANDER   Enough, Leonides,
You go beyond the praise. We have our end,
And all is ended well. We have now seen
The flowers and weeds* that grew about our court.

SIMONIDES   [*Aside, looking at his ornate attire*]
If these be weeds, I'm afraid I shall wear none so   680
good again as long as my father lives.

EVANDER   Only this gentlemen we did abuse

649 *myriad* ten thousand
670 *viands* provisions
680 *weeds* garments

With our own bosom; we seemed a tyrant
And he, our instrument. Look, 'tis Cratilus,
[*The executioner takes off his hood*]
The man that you supposed had now been travelled,   695
Which we gave leave to learn to speak
And bring us foreign languages to Greece.
All's joyed, I see. Let music be the crown
And set this high: "The good needs fear no law,
It is his safety, and the bad man's awe."   700
[*Flourish. Exeunt omnes*]

699 *this* ed. (it Q)

NOTES TO THE TEXT

Act I, scene i

p.4 1.31 *two of three score* There is some confusion as
to Antigona's age. Here Simonides indicates she is
fifty-eight; later in the scene (I.i.296) Creon says
she is "scarce fifty-five" and Antigona herself
refers to her "five remaining years" (I.i.298).
Finally, in Act II, Simonides calls her "seven-and-
fifty" (II.i.166). Assuming Antigona and Creon
would most likely be accurate, Gifford may be right
that "Sim's impatience of his mother's death leads
him to error."

p.5 1.54 *seven-fold sages* of Greece were Thales, Solon,
Periander, Cleobulus, Chilon, Bias, and Pittacus; all
lived about the 6th and 7th centuries B.C. To each
was attributed some wise maxim by ancient writers
(OED).

p.5 1.59 *Draco* (perhaps 621/20 B.C.) was an Athenian
lawmaker known for the severity of his penalties.
When asked why he specified death as the penalty for
most offences, he replied that small offences deserved death and he knew of no severer penalty for
great ones (OCD).

p.5 1.61 *Solon* (c 574-3 B.C.) was an Athenian statesman
appointed to resolve the legislative crisis which had
arisen from the severe conditions of serfdom. One of
his first acts was chreokopia (OCD). (see glossary
1.61)

p.5 1.65 *Areopagitae* originally referred to the council
of advisors to the king who took their name from the
Hill of Ares, northwest of the Acropolis in Athens.
As the monarchy declined, however, it was probably,
by the 7th century B.C., virtually in charge of government. Solon (see notes 1.61) set down its constitutional powers in writing and so perhaps somewhat limited them (OCD). As indicated here, their
powers were primarily judicial.

p. 5 1.66-77 *Lysurgus was . . . their shame.* Having
referred to two famous Athenians, Draco and Solon,

who made statutory changes to improve the political
welfare of the state, the second lawyer now goes on
to three whose dictates were designed to improve the
physical well-being of the state: Lycurgus, Plato,
and Aristotle. Their errors, according to him, lay
in their interest in methods of breeding rather than
pruning the populace after predecided length of life
as Evander does by his new edict.

p.5   1.66 *Lycurgus* (c 390-c 325-4) King and law-maker of
Lacedaemonia noted for being mercilessly severe in
his prosecutions. In describing his regulations
governing marriage, Plutarch says, "For example, an
elderly man with a young wife, if he look with favour
and esteem on some fair and noble young man, might
introduce him to her, and adopt her offspring by
such a noble father as his own. And again, a worthy
man who admired some woman for the fine children that
she bore her husband and the modesty of her behaviour
as a wife, might enjoy her favours, if her husband
would consent, thus planting, as it were, in a soil
of beautiful fruitage, and begetting for himself
noble sons. . . . The freedom which thus prevailed at
that time in marriage relations was aimed at physical
and political well-being, and was far removed from
the licentiousness which was afterwards attributed to
their women. . . ." (*Lives* with an English translation by Bernadotte Perrin [London, 1914] I, 251-2).

p.5   1.71 *Plato* (c 429-347 B.C.) Athenian philosopher
and teacher who in *The Republic* has Socrates say,
"Women of this kind [having the qualities of a
guardian], then, must be selected to cohabit with men
of this kind. . . . And on the young men, surely, who
excel in war and other pursuits we must bestow
honours and prizes, and, in particular, the oppor-
tunity of more frequent intercourse with the women,
which will at the same time be a plausible pretext
for having them beget as many of the children as
possible." "That is the condition, he [Glaucon] said,
"Of preserving the purity of the guardians' breed."
(with an English translation by Paul Shorey [London,
1930] I, 449, 463).

p.5   1.72 *Aristotle* (384-322 B.C.) Greek philosopher and
teacher who was a student at Plato's school in Athens.
In Book VII of *Politics*, he says, "Inasmuch therefore

as it is the duty of the lawgiver to consider from
the start how the children reared are to obtain the
best bodily frames, he must first pay attention to
the union of the sexes, and settle when and in what
condition a couple should practice matrimonial intercourse." His emphasis is obviously on "matrimonial
intercourse" for later he proscribes, "As to intercourse with another man or woman, in general it must
be dishonourable for them to be known to take any
part in it in any circumstances whatsoever as long as
they are husband and wife and bear those names, but
any who may be discovered doing anything of the sort
during their period of parenthood must be punished
with a loss of privilege suited to the offence" (with
an English translation by H. Rackham [London, 1932]
pp. 617, 625). The "lewd and luxurious laws" to
which the second lawyer refers are probably those
governing the exposing of children that are born de-
formed and the aborting of women found pregnant in
contravention of any of the regulations laid down by
the state (*Ibid* p. 623).

p.7 1.112 *It is no rule . . . to punish.* Considering
the continuation of the conversation and the lawyers'
sophistical argument on what in fact constitutes in-
nocence (11. 125-133), recall of the massacre of the
innocents (Matthew ii: 16) may be intended. Thus the
edict of Evander which is upheld by the book of birth
registration from which legal age can be discerned is
equated with the law of Herod whereas Cleanthes' concept of justuce is upheld by the law of Moses,
"Honour thy father and thy mother" (Exodus xx: 12;
Deuteronomy v: 16), from Holy Writ.

p.12 11.228-31 *Forty of 'em . . . Napping now.* The
meaning of this passage is somewhat obscure but is
obviously meant to be sardonic (see Antigona's response 1. 234). The phrase *due deeds of darkness* is
perhaps a play on "Give the devil his due (*Tilley*
D273)" and "Give everyone his due" (*Tilley* D643).
Thus, 'The elderly men have, to give them credit,
done much service for which their country appeared
to honour them. Now, however, it has turned on them
when they least expected it' ("caught them napping"
Tilley N36-7). (See also I *Hen* VI.ii.i.38, Had this
their watch been good, This sudden mischief could not
have fall'n.)

p.12 1.246 *winter* ed. (winters Q) *sicknesses* those ill-
nesses common to the cold time of the year. Perhaps
proverbial; 1611 Cot., s. v. Passer: A mortall foe
he scapes who scapes a Winters day (*Tilley* W513).

p.14 11.293-5 *She has a . . . to her longest thread.*
The new edict seeks to take from nature a right that
is inherently hers - to decide a life's span. Therefore nature will retaliate by extending life as long
as she can.

p.14 1.296 *Thou art scarce fifty-five* See I.i. 31n

p.16 1.334 *five years hence* See I.i. 31n and 296n

p.17 11.351-7 *Improvident . . . die within 'em.* This is an
appeal by Cleanthes to Nature to reform man and make
him live up to those potentials of love and loyalty
of which having a soul makes him capable; potentials
which lower forms of life do not have.

p.18 11.374-5 *Why . . . my debted duty.* Hippolita's
love, though it does not stem from a direct blood
relationship, appears greater than Cleanthes'.

p.19 11.405-6 *A daughter-in-law? . . . such children.*
Hippolita, whose ties are by statutory law, is
proving more devoted than many bound by natural law.
Simonides and other of the courtiers, on the other
hand, are using statutory law to violate the ties of
natural law.

p.22 11.501-6 *Why, there's . . . no second?* Cleanthes
means that as he and Hippolita are one by marriage
and he and his father are one by blood, therefore the
three form one unit, one "counsel."

Act II, scene i

p.25 1.30 *in two-penny commons* In the Henslowe papers
concerning the building of the Globe (*Henslowe's
Diary*, ed. 1961, p. 308), there is reference to the
provision for "gentlemans rooms and two penny rooms."
Thus, here the courtier is complaining about being
able to afford only public accommodations, not
private.

p.26 11.54-6 *To arraign . . . whisper.* There is a
deliberate irony here; first in the use of legal
terminology and, second, in the courtier's accusation
of the old men's avarice.

p.28 11.101-3 *and he . . . well after* This aphorism,
with its proverbial overtones (He that serves God
serves a good master [*Tilley* G235]), reinforces the
main conflict of the play -- service to the Maker of
holy writ vs. service to the maker of secular law.

p.28 1.114 *seven Christian kingdoms* These were England,
Scotland, Ireland, Wales, France, Italy, and Spain.
Each had its champion: George, Andrew, Patrick, David,
Denis, Anthony, and James. Richard Johnson's romance,
*The Most Famous History of the Seven Champions of
Chistendom,* published in 1596, was so enormously
popular that Johnson added a second part in 1608 and
a third in 1616. The ballad, "A Brave Warlike Song,"
which recites the names of these nations and their
champions in its refrain, probably appeared in print
first in 1626 but there is certainly no reason to
assume it had not been popularly sung before that
date (see *The Pepys Ballads,* ed. Hyder Edward Rollins,
[Harvard: 1929] II, 54).

p.30 11.146-7 *Save . . . cheese-trenchers* Bullen points
out the frequent allusions by old authors to the
"practice of inscribing posies on cheese-trenchers.
(see Middleton's *No Wit, No Help like a Woman's* II.i
[60-69])."

p.30 11.148-9 *Take heed . . . runnet* Cheese-rennet is
the name given for the plant *galium verum* because of
its properties for curdling milk. However, the plant
is also called Lady's Bedstraw and thus Simonides
converts the aphorism into a bawdy pun. Ironically,
the saying proscribes in other words the Commandment,
"Thou shalt not commit adultery."

p.30 1.162 *cast down* Again Simonides is punning.
Antigona has but a few years before she too will become a victim of the edict and be "cast down" from
the promontory (see 11. 157-8). Therefore, says
Simonides, she should use the time well and allow
herself to be "cast down" upon her back to enjoy a
young courtier.

p.30 11.166-7 See I.i.31n; I.i.296n.

p.32 11.192-4 *I ha[ve] known . . . rain in sunshine*
Proverbial; see c1520 Walter *Spectacle Lovers* in
Collier *Bibliog. Acct.*, IV 212; Full harde it is to
fynde a woman stedfast, For yf one eye wepe the other
contrary (*Tilley* E248).

p. 32 11.207-23 *It grieves me . . . entirely merry.*
This whole passage plays the changes upon the deceit
and dissembling inherent within the passage above
(11. 192-4). (See also c1526 *Dicta Sap.*, s.C4: The
wepying of an heire is dissembed laughyng, yea he
reioyceth though he wepe; 1615 Welde *Janua Ling.* 190,
p. 12: The weeping of an heire, in laughter vnder a
maske [*Tilley* E248]).

p.33 11.228-9 *Sorrow's a thief . . . forth a grief.* This
sounds proverbial and may be connected with Spenser
Shep. Cal. May 1.152: "Sorrowe ne neede be hastened
on: For he will come, without calling, anone." A
similar idea is expressed later 1639CL., s.v. Risus,
p. 274: 'Sorrow is laughter's daughter' (see *Tilley*
S654, 658).

p.33 1.242 *He that brought . . . to clay.* Although the
narrative meaning of this sentence is clear, biblical
overtones were probably intended (see Genesis ii:17;
Job xxx:6)

p.34 11.257-8 *They will eat . . . munching!* Simonides
means that even if he employed more servants than
these six, there would still not be enough to look
after his wardrobe.

p.35 1.285 *slash-me* This refers to the latest fashion in
men's clothes. The slash was a vertical slit made in
a garment in order to expose to view a lining or
under garment of different or contrasting colour
(OED).

p.35 1.296 *And I'll firk some too.* This is another of
Simonides' bawdy puns. *Firk* here means a quick cut
or thrust and the *some* refers to some whores (see
1611 Cotgrave, *Bichecoterie: . .* firkerie, an odde
pranke, or jerke, in whoorism [*Obs.* OED]); perhaps
cognate with fig, feague, an Elizabethan obscenity.

p.36 1.298 *or it shall cost hot water.* Proverbial; c1538
Lisle Papers, p. 423: If they be to be had, I will
have of them, or it shall cost me hot water (*Tilley*
W97).

p.36 11.299-300 *scald the devil* infect the devil with
a venereal disease (Partridge); or, perhaps 'purify
the devil in hell-fire.' The term scalding-house
was a euphemism for hell (*Obs.* OED). Thus the cook
may be suggesting that in an age which denies a man
his honest profession, anything can happen.

p.37 11.310-11 *Oracle Butler!* . . . *of the name!* This is
a topical jest referring to Dr. William Butler (1535-
1618), an eccentric London physician of amazing
reputation and noted for unusual prescriptions and
practices during the second decade of the 17th
century. Although his reputation continued for some
years after his death January 18, 1618 (see DNB), it
is unlikely that a theatre audience could be expected
to pick up the jest for more than a year or so after
the death. Thus, this reference may be cited as
evidence for *The Old Law* having been written c1618-19.

Act II scene ii

p.38 1.11 *dogdays* the days about the time of the
heliacal rising of the Dog-star; noted from ancient
times as the hottest and most unwholesome period of
the year (OED)

p.35 11.35-7 *The sweetbriar's* . . . *lady.* Here again the
humour is dependent upon the bawdy inuendo.

p.39 1.39 *performed* This may be a reference to the
courtiers' entrance in which they probably perform a
sweeping gesture with their hats. For some reason,
Bullen and Gifford prefer "perfumed."

p.40 11.60-1 *he that loves* . . . *a widow well.* This may
be merely another bawdy comment or it may be Proverbial; A grunting horse and a groaning wife seldom
fail their master (*Tilley* H649).

p.41 1.82 *Alas, poor ghost!* see *Hamlet* I.v.4

p.43 1.119 *for other!* for another part of her body than her hands

Act III scene i

p.48 1.25 *I take . . . Bollux.* Gnotho is punning that Pollux did not make a very good job of his progeny (Agatha); he 'made a ballocks of it,' or 'made a balls of it.'

p.48 1.29 *Born . . . 'tis '99.* This line has been cited to indicate that *The Old Law* was written in 1599. Modern scholars have disproved this early date and suggest that the playwrights chose figures that would allow the audience easy calculation of Agatha's age.

p.51 11.101-2 *'Tis done . . . black and white.* By the change of Agatha's birth date to 1539, the church registry now sets her age at 60 and, therefore, she is subject to the new edict.

p.51 11.107-8 *Asses have ears as well as pitchers* Proverbial; Small (little) pitchers have wide ears (*Tilley* P363). Asses (the approaching servants), of course, have even wider ears.

p.51. 11.109-11 *Here's a trick . . . lived.* "This alludes to those games, in which the low cards were thrown out; *coats* were what we call court [face] cards," Gifford.

p.51 1.112 *And is this then the end of serving men?* "is the title of an old ballad," Gifford. "An allusion to the old ballad," Bullen. Extensive search has not turned up the ballad to which these editors refer. In correspondence with the editor, Professors Bertrand Bronson (University of California, Berkley) and Claude Simpson (Stanford) were both willing to accept my conjecture that the line may have occurred at the climactic point of an earlier variant of "The Famous Flower of Serving Men" (Childe no. 1-6).

p.60 11.357-8 *The clerk . . . forward already* Hebrew is written from right to left on the page.

Act III, scene ii

p.70 l.201 *I'll pay you speedily____ ____, with a trick*
Space is left here for the actor to include any
obscene expletives which come to his mind.

Act IV, scene i

p.77 ll.14-16 *What! . . . needs be flyblown.* The coarse
repartee of this dialogue is probably based on an
earlier version of the vulgarism 'to put four quarters on the spit' meaning to have sexual intercourse
(see Partridge p. 810).

p.77 ll.50-2 *But the heads . . . gitternheads.* There is
obviously jovial insult intended here. Hogshead is
self-explanatory; citternheaded meant having a gro-
tesque head such as those often carved on a cittern
(see OED)

p.77 ll.56-7 *No dancing . . . the fair Greek, man.* These
two lines are designed to play upon a tag from a lost
play of George Peele's *The Turkish Mahamet and Hyrin
[Irene] the Fair Greek* (1581-94). Dramatic varia-
tions of the line "Have we not Siren [Hiren] here"
appear in 1597 Shakespeare *2H IV*, II.iv.145; 1601
Dekker *Satiromastix*, IV.iii.243-4; 1604 Day *Law
Tricks*, Malone Society, ll. 1330-1; 1605 Jonson,
Chapman, Marston *Eastward Ho* V.ii.107-8 and others.
The name Hyrin (Hyren, Hiren) became synonymous with
harlot. In *Merrie Conceited Jests of George Peele*
(1607), not by the playwright but a compilation of
tricks supposedly ascribed to him, there appears in
"How George read a Play-booke to a Gentleman," re-
ference to "the famous play of the Turkish Mahamet.
And Hyrin the faire Greeke, in the Italian called a
Curtezan, in Spaine, a Margerite, in French un Cur-
tain, in England among the barbarous a whore: but
among the Gentle their usuall associates a punke:
. . ." (B4v). Or, again, in Thomas Adams' sermon,
"The Spiritual Navigator" (1615), he says, "There be
Sirens in the *Sea* of this *world. Syrens? Hirens,* as
they are now called . . . . What a number of these
Siren, Hirens, Cockatrices, Couteghians, in plaine
English *Harlots* swimme amongst vs, happy it is for
him that hath only heard, and not beene infected"

p. 28. In *The Old Law*, Gnotho's low comic repetition
of the names and of the tag itself (see ll. 99 , 106,
116) would each occasion further bursts of coarse
laughter.

p.80 ll.76-7 *When she grew . . . by a quarter.* This
vulgar rejoinder means that when she grew to be an
ell [45 inches] she was deeper by a quarter[9 inches]
than any yard [36 inches]; penis could reach.

p.80 ll.82-4 *True . . . holes with.* This coarse rejoinder of Gnotho's also relies upon audience association
of Helen of Troy with harlotry (see above 1. 67).

p.83 ll.153-4, 157 *and then thou die'st for adultery . .
. . Oh, you'd be stoned to death would you?* (see
Leviticus xx:10, Deuteronomy xxii:24, then John
viii:4 "And say unto him, Master, this woman was
taken in adultery, in the very act," and viii:5 "Now
Moses in the Law commanded us, that such should be
stoned: what sayest thou.") There is great irony
here that Gnotho, of all people, should be citing
the law of Moses.

p.83 ll.169-71 *Go . . . out of date!* According to
Eustace F. Bosanquet (Intro. to *English Printed Al-
manacks and Prognostications,* 1917, p. 32), Anthony
Askham [Ascham, DNB] (fl.1553) was the first English
almanac writer to begin his year in January "and this
example was followed by most of the English Prognos-
ticators." Thus, Gnotho is equating Agatha to an
almanac which has almost outlived its usefulness.

p.84 ll.172-4 *sell some . . . bawds do so much* Rings
embellished with the figure of a human skull were
commonly worn on the middle finger by whores and
procuresses.

p.84 1.176 *old stock fish* the parenthetical note added
by the OED "often with reference to the beating of
the fish before cooking," may link Gnotho's remark
to the stoning threatened above (1. 160).

p.84 ll.190-2 *I'll plague thee . . . afterward!* "It was
a common superstition that ghosts haunted the spot
where in their lifetime they had concealed treasure."
Bullen

Act IV, Scene ii

p.86 1.43 *I find 'em . . . legions* (see Matthew xxvi:53
Thinkest thou that I cannot pray to my father, and
he shall presently give me more than twelve legions
of angels).

p.91 11.166-7 *He has the lapwing's . . . nest.* Proverbial; The lapwing cries most when furthest from
her nest (reference cited in *Tilley* L68).

p.96 11.312-3 *You'll prove . . . are married.* The word
for which *cut* stands in this line was considered,
even in the 17th C, particularly vulgar; thus, the
line is perhaps the most obscene in the play. Literally it means, 'You'll prove a bawdy unchaste,
lewd bachelor, Sim, to have a cut [female pudend]
upon your finger [penis] before you're married.'
(see Shakespeare *TN* II.v.95-9 and the Induction to
Marston's *The Malcontent*, 11,34-7)

Act V, scene I

p.102 11.112-3 *He hath left . . . white again.* Proverbial;
He has eaten a snake (reference cited in *Tilley* S584)
(For the meaning see 1580 Lyly *Euph. and His Eng.*,
p. 134: Therfore hath it grown to a Prouerb in Italy,
when one see-eth a woman striken in age to look
amiable, he saith she hath eaten a Snake; 1666
Toriano *Prov. Phr.*, s.v. Serpi, p. 190: To look as if
one had eaten Snakes, viz. to look young again.)

p.106 11.219-28 *Where's that Aeneas . . . save a father.*
In Book II of Virgil's *Aeneid*, Dido of Carthage asks
Aeneas to tell of the misfortunes of Troy at the
hands of the Greeks. In the course of his relation,
Aeneas describes how he was bid by Venus to save his
family from the sack and conflagration which destroyed the Trojan city. Although he lost his wife,
Creusa, in the confusion, Virgil's hero, with his
son by the hand and his father, Anchises, on his
back, struggled through burning Troy to safety.

p.112 1.405 *Enter clowne . . . the wedding.* In the Q
there is a duplication of stage directions here. The
second set has been retained since it is obviously
a revision from the first and the clearest indication

of the intended make-up of the procession.

p.113 ll.425-6 *Will it . . . courtesy?* At this point,
Gnotho may be gesturing toward the wedding cake or
toward Siren or, of course, with a sweeping gesture
toward both.

p.114 l.432 *remedy doloris* In Philip Barrough's *The
Method of Physic* (London: 1583) "moderate carnal
copulation" is cited as a cure for melancholy (p.46).

p.119 ll.559-64 *Oh music! . . . no bedding.* This speech
is an extended parody of Hieronimo's speech, "O eyes,
no eyes, but fountains fraught with tears;/O life,
no life, but lively form of death" (Kyd *Spanish
Tragedy* III.ii.1ff).

p.119 ll.573-4 *No more . . . dishes!* Proverbial; He gets
by that as Dickens did by his distress [dishes].
(reference cited in ODEP; see also 1579 R. Gallis
*A Brief Treatise contayning the Cruelty of Elizabeth
Style*, "I was constrained to take half the money they
cost mee gaining by them as Dickens did by his Dishes
who bying fiue for twopence solde six for a penny.")

p.121 l.626 *The elephants have found their joints too.*
Supposedly Ctesias, a 5th Century Greek doctor saw
and described an elephant as having no knee joints.
Although this error was later denied by Aristotle,
the idea became interpolated into various other
fables concerning elephants. (See 1535 *The Dialoges
of Creatures Moralysed*, dial. lxxxix: This beaste
is very famows and greately renomyd, amonge all
other beasties, and notwithstondinge he may not
knele, for he hath no kneys; see also 1604 Chapman
All Fools, V.ii.65: 1606 Shakespeare *Troil.* II.iii.
104-5; 1633 Rowley *All's Lost by Lust*, II.i.83) The
issue was disputed by Sir Thomas Browne in *Pseudo-
doxia Epidemica* (1646) Book III, Chapt. 1 and the
idea appears as "The elephant sleeps standing" in
Torriano's *Piazza Universale di Proverbe Italiani*
(1666) p. 80.

p.122 l.712 *flowers and weeds* a metaphor for the true
courtiers and the false.